The Fall
and Rise of the
ISLAMIC
STATE

The Fall and Rise of the
ISLAMIC STATE

NOAH FELDMAN

WITH A NEW INTRODUCTION BY THE AUTHOR

A Council on Foreign Relations Book

PRINCETON UNIVERSITY PRESS

PRINCETON AND OXFORD

Copyright © 2008 by Noah Feldman
Published by Princeton University Press, 41 William Street,
Princeton, New Jersey 08540
In the United Kingdom: Princeton University Press, 6 Oxford Street,
Woodstock, Oxfordshire OX20 1TW

press.princeton.edu

ALL RIGHTS RESERVED

First printing, 2008
First paperback printing, 2010
Paperback reissue, with a new introduction by the author, 2012
Paperback ISBN 978-0-691-15624-8

The Library of Congress has cataloged the previous edition of this book as follows

Feldman, Noah, 1970–
The fall and rise of the Islamic state / Noah Feldman.
p.   cm.
"A Council on Foreign Relations Book."
Includes bibliographical references and index.
ISBN 978-0-691-12045-4 (hardcover : alk. paper)
1. Islam and state. 2. Constitutional law (Islamic law) 3. Islamic law—
Political aspects. 4. Islamic countries—Politics and government. I. Title.
KBP2000.F45   2008
340.5′9—dc22   2007047918

British Library Cataloging-in-Publication Data is available

The Council on Foreign Relations is an independent, nonpartisan membership organization, think tank, and publisher dedicated to being a resource for its members, government officials, business executives, journalists, educators and students, civic and religious leaders, and other interested citizens in order to help them better understand the world and the foreign policy choices facing the United States and other countries. Founded in 1921, the Council carries out its mission by maintaining a diverse membership, with special programs to promote interest and develop expertise in the next generation of foreign policy leaders; convening meetings at its headquarters in New York and in Washington, DC, and other cities where senior government officials, members of Congress, global leaders, and prominent thinkers come together with Council members to discuss and debate major international issues; supporting a Studies Program that fosters independent research, enabling Council scholars to produce articles, reports, and books and hold roundtables that analyze foreign policy issues and make concrete policy recommendations; publishing *Foreign Affairs*, the preeminent journal on international affairs and U.S. foreign policy; sponsoring Independent Task Forces that produce reports with both findings and policy prescriptions on the most important foreign policy topics; and providing up-to-date information and analysis about world events and American foreign policy on its website, CFR.org.

This book has been composed in Minion Typeface
Printed on acid-free paper. ∞
Printed in the United States of America
1 3 5 7 9 10 8 6 4 2

In memory of Muhsin Mahdi, 1926–2007

The order, the discipline, the temporal and spiritual ambition of the clergy, are unknown to the Moslems; and the sages of the law are the guides of their conscience and the oracle of their faith. From the Atlantic to the Ganges the Koran is acknowledged as the fundamental code, not only of theology but of civil and criminal jurisprudence; and the laws which regulate the actions and the property of mankind are guarded by the infallible and immutable sanction of the will of God.

Gibbon, *The Decline and Fall of the Roman Empire*,
chap. 50 (5:325)

The scholars are the heirs of the prophets.
Sunan Abi Dawud, book 25:3634

CONTENTS

INTRODUCTION TO
THE 2012 EDITION

A DECADE AGO, with the memory of the attacks of September 11 still fresh, some found it quixotic to suggest that the long-term trend of political Islam was toward a complex synthesis with constitutional democracy. But in a 2003 book, *After Jihad*, I argued exactly that. I drew my evidence from the unexpected success of Islamists in the quickly reversed Algerian elections of 1991; from the writings of prominent exiled Islamists like the Tunisian intellectual Rachid Ghannouchi and the Egyptian television-imam Yusuf al-Qaradawi; and above all from the way Islamism had defined itself against secular autocracy.

What I lacked were concrete examples of electoral success and constitution writing by political parties made up of what I called Islamic democrats. The Turkish Justice and Development Party, or AKP, was new to power and untested. It was clearly inspired by Islam, yet constrained by political norms that insisted on formal secularism. In Afghanistan, the U.S.-backed government that inherited power from the Taliban was still feeling its way to a constitutional *loya jirga* that would somehow try to accommodate democratic and Islamic norms. Most troubling, in the Arabic-speaking world, regimes could be divided into monarchies and dictatorships—but all looked impervious to domestic overthrow by democratic means. Where, I asked, was the Muslim equivalent to the Solidarity movement that helped overthrow communism in Poland? Islamism clearly expressed an aspiration to better forms of self-government. But the possibilities for exploring them were blocked by repressive governments that had for decades been highly effective in preserving their positions.

Five years later, in 2008, when I wrote the book that you now hold in your hands, history had provided more evidence for democratic tendencies within Islamism—but also new bases to identify the challenges that Islamic constitutional democracy would confront when it was put into action. In Afghanistan and Iraq, democratic forces unleashed after the United States removed existing regimes had given rise to Islamic democratic constitutionalism. The governments in Kabul and Baghdad were struggling, to be sure. But when the public in these countries had been given the opportunity to select politicians who would create new constitutions for them, their preferences had been relatively clear. Each had chosen a constitutional path that sought to combine Islam—encapsulated by shariʿa, the classical Islamic law—with constitutional democracy. Meanwhile, the call for an Islamic state was only rising throughout the Muslim world.

My goals in writing this book were to explain where that call originated; to offer an interpretation of Islamic constitutional history that emphasized constitutional balance and the rule of law; to suggest how late Ottoman reforms gave rise to autocracy; and to sketch the profound challenges that would face the constitution drafters of new Islamic states. In writing the book, I faced once again a serious limitation: my leading examples of Islamic constitutionalism had emerged only in the context of conquest and occupation. I could demonstrate that the political programs adopted by Islamists all over the Arabic-speaking world emphasized the rule of law and just, democratic government. But I had no examples of a free and unencumbered public choosing Islamic democrats and putting the job of constitution drafting in their hands. I believed my analysis was correct; but an unsympathetic reader could still question my most basic claims simply by invoking the Taliban and declaring that shari'a could not possibly provide the basis for the rule of law.

Then came the Arab Spring. Beginning in early 2011, large, spontaneous public outpourings of democratic feeling began to spread from North Africa to Yemen, Syria and Bahrain—a geographical range that spanned the Arabic-speaking world. In Tunisia and Egypt, which presented two classic models of secular autocracy, long-stable governments fell of their own accord when the military refused to support the repression of public protest. As spring turned into summer and fall, Libya's secular dictator, the notorious Muammar Qaddafi, was challenged by regional protest and rebellion, then brought down by a sustained Western bombing campaign designed to bring the rebels to power. As the year came to a close, Yemen's dictator was eventually forced to pass political authority to his vice president. In Syria, the second-generation secular dictatorship of Bashar al-Assad was locked in a violent and growing civil conflict that threatened to become an all-out civil war.

The consequences of these upheavals were extraordinarily significant for the question of the Islamic constitutional state. Tunisia, where the Arab Spring began, forms the most straightforward example. Deeply influenced by a leftist, postcolonial revolutionary tradition and an ongoing French influence among its elite political class, it might easily have been described as the most secular Arab country of them all. The weekend there takes place on Saturday and Sunday, as it does in Europe, not on Friday, the traditional Muslim day of public communal gathering. At the height of Tunisian secularism, Habib Bourguiba, the independence leader turned president, caused the Islamic scholars, or 'ulama, to declare that one need not fast during Ramadan because the work of building the state substituted for this basic pillar of Islamic religious practice. If Tunisia could become the home of an Islamic democracy, then the power of the trend could be proven once and for all.

To understand the trajectory of contemporary Islamic constitutionalism in Tunisia, one must begin by observing that Tunisia's Islamists did not start the Arab Spring. The protests against the dictatorship began spontaneously when a frustrated fruit seller named Mohamed Bouazizi set himself on fire after a humiliating encounter with a police officer. The protests spread via trade unions and, eventually, middle-class young people frustrated with political injustice and limited economic opportunities. The leading Tunisian Islamist political organization, Ennahda, took no role—and for good reason. Since running a few unofficial candidates for office in 1989, the group had been banned and its members imprisoned or exiled. Any organization that the movement might have had within Tunisia was underground. Rachid Ghannouchi, its leading figure, had been outside the country for twenty years.

Nor did the Islamists play a significant part in bringing down the Ben Ali regime. The key role here was played by the military, to whom the government turned when police were inadequate to put down the crowds of hundreds of thousands who had begun to gather in cities that included the capital, Tunis.

The calculus that the military had to make was a subtle one—and it would be repeated, with variations, in Egypt. On the one hand was the devil it knew: a familiar regime led by an aging dictator. Even if order could be restored and the protesters made to go home through a show of force, Zine El Abidine Ben Ali, who had ruled since 1987, was seventy-five years old. A transition loomed. And yet Tunisia had no well-established mechanism for transition, either hereditary or democratic. Ben Ali was only the second president Tunisia had ever had, and he had come to power in a coup d'état that replaced the resistance hero Bourguiba after thirty years in office.

On the other hand was uncertainty. The military judged correctly that it lacked the legitimacy to take power itself, at least with the population in the streets calling for democratic reforms. The consequence of the military choosing to abandon Ben Ali would be a caretaker government followed by elections. Instead of being seen as the iron fist of a fading dictator, the military would be heralded by the crowd as the midwife of democracy. Its institutional legitimacy would be preserved, indeed enhanced, for generations to come.

In the end, the decision was not especially difficult. The commander of the army announced that his troops would protect the revolution. That day, Ben Ali was on a plane out of the country. After some uncertainty about the precise form of the transition, a consensus government of mostly secular moderates was formed until elections for a constituent assembly could be held. The entire process was relatively peaceful, a democratic triumph of the type familiar from the so-called color revolutions of Eastern Europe. Banned political parties were allowed to register. The stage was set for a free, democratic election in an Arab country—without a de facto foreign occupation in place at the same time.

It was in the electoral process and its aftermath that the Islamists entered the fray. Whatever insecurity they may have felt about the fact that the revolution had taken place without them was quickly assuaged by public enthusiasm for their program. Ghannuchi returned from exile as a hero. His distinctive brand of Islamic democracy, developed over many years of theoretical reflection and writing, became the basis for the official political platform of Tunisia's Islamist political party, Ennahda. Critics had long disparaged abstract claims to the effect that Islam and democracy were in principle compatible. Ghannuchi's emphasis on equality of women and non-Muslims in an Islamic state was dismissed as pure rhetoric. His argument that shariʿa ideals could provide a moral bulwark for democratic constitutionalism was challenged as unrealistic. Now the public was being given a chance to decide what it believed.

Measured by electoral results, the public response was overwhelming. The liberal secularist professionals who had led the revolution seemed to gain little credibility from their efforts. Ennahda won 37 percent of the seats in the new constituent assembly. The next-largest party received just under 9 percent. Even taken collectively, the four largest vote getters after Ennahda took less than 26 percent of the vote, with the remainder split among multiple small parties or unaffiliated representatives. Superior organization no doubt helped lead Ennahda to its victory. But the scope made it clear that support had everything to do with an active preference for Ennahda's highly specific constitutional vision of Islamic democracy. This was not just an ordinary election for who would govern, but a once-in-a-lifetime opportunity to choose the people who would write the new Tunisian constitution. For this task, the public embraced Islamic democracy: and the challenge was set.

As of this writing, that constitutional process is still under way. Although Ennahda seems to have agreed to omit any explicit mention of shariʿa from the constitution, various proposals analyzed later in this book are being considered and discussed, relating both to the question of shariʿa as a source of law and to the possibility of what I call Islamic judicial review. The challenges that Ennahda will face, both in writing a new constitution and in governing subsequently, will be enormous. In particular, as I argue in this book, the party will have to confront the deep problem of how to generate constitutional balance in a political culture that has not known it since the period of colonial rule. The mere invocation of Islam cannot create constitutional balance. Real institutions need to emerge that are capable of balancing one another in order to generate stable and effective political governance. Political parties are part of the institutional development that must occur, but they are far from sufficient—especially when their sizes are out of balance. The military, too, may potentially play some role—but that is another story. In particular, it is the story that is emerging in the second of the successful Arab Spring revolutions, that of Egypt.

⊗

If Tunisia has historically been a minor player in the Arab world, small in size and an outlier in terms of secularism, Egypt has, in the modern era, been at the very heart of Arab self-consciousness. Not only is Egypt by far the most populous Arab country, and the most geographically central, but it is also the home of the two great competing ideological movements of the last Arab century: Arab nationalism and political Islam. It is Egypt that saw the first glimmerings of Arab liberal constitutionalism in the waning days of British colonial control; and Egypt that saw that liberalism destroyed when ineffectual, brief constitutional monarchy was brought down by military coup. Gamal Abdel Nasser, the colonel who emerged as Egypt's undisputed leader, became (by self-proclamation) the voice of the Arab nation. He set the basic terms of presidential dictatorship in the Arab world that would be followed by Hafez al-Assad, Saddam Hussein, Qaddafi, and many others.

Almost from the moment it began, the peaceful, democratic uprising in Egypt overshadowed the Tunisian movement that inspired it. Tahrir Square, a vast and generally rather desolate expanse in the middle of downtown Cairo, near the Egypt Museum, had the capacity to hold a million or more people. And often, during those extraordinary weeks and months of 2011, it did.

Beginning with middle- and upper-middle-class young people who coordinated their movements with the new mass technology of instant messaging, the gathering in the square gradually extended its demographic reach. By the end, a reasonable cross-section of Egyptian society could be found demanding an end to Hosni Mubarak's regime. Television and mobile-phone cameras alike captured the scene, which inspired viewers throughout the Arabic-speaking world. If Egypt's self-conception as the leader of the Arab world had faltered during the previous thirty years, Tahrir Square revived this vision and restored Egypt's political soul to consciousness.

As in Tunisia, however, the Islamists remained in the background. Pious Muslims could be found in the square, but the Muslim Brotherhood, the flagship organization of Sunni Islamism, took no official role in the demonstrations for several months. Once outlawed and suppressed by the government, the Brotherhood had, in recent years, been involved in a subtle movement toward respectability and limited political participation. It had run candidates for office without officially identifying them as representatives of the movement. And it had a detailed political program that could be read by anybody with access to its pamphlets or the Internet. But it did not choose to ride the initial wave of democratic dissent.

The Brotherhood's motives for caution were multiple. One was surely that it did not want to jeopardize its privileged position as an unrecognized but potent political opposition. Had the protests been successfully suppressed and their participants delegitimized, the Brotherhood would have hoped to avoid being tarred with the brush of rebellion.

Another worry was more subtle and yet probably more significant. The organized presence of representatives of the Muslim Brotherhood in the square would open to the regime the possibility of claiming before the international community that the rising against it was inspired by religious fundamentalism. From painful experience, the Brotherhood understood that the West was deeply concerned about Islamist political mobilization. As the Mubarak regime struggled for international support to maintain its increasingly tenuous hold on power, the Brotherhood worried that it might be aiding the enemy by becoming identified with the Arab Spring.

Eventually, however, the tipping point was reached. The Brotherhood was forced to acknowledge that continued silence in the presence of such a significant democracy movement would look like acquiescence in the survival of the regime. That would not only have been bad for the Brotherhood; it would have called into question the Brotherhood's nearly century-old legacy of opposition to monarchic and dictatorial regimes. By the time the Islamists entered the square, the regime seemed doomed to fail. The game was already to influence the form of government that would emerge in the aftermath of regime change.

Unlike Ben Ali in Tunisia, however, Mubarak balked at the thought of exile. The popular outpouring of opposition was not, on its own, enough to remove him from office. Tear gas and bullets deployed by police forces and the intelligence services were not enough to send the protesters home. The stalemate put the balance of power in the hands of the army.

After a period of indecision, the army took matters into its own hands. On the evening of February 10, 2011, Mubarak went on national television and insisted that he would remain as head of state. The next day, February 11, the vice president announced that Mubarak was no longer in office—and that the country was in the hands of Egypt's Supreme Council of Armed Forces, or SCAF. This was a coup d'état, albeit one accomplished against the backdrop of popular and democratic protest. It opened the door for a lengthy—and still continuing—period of complex power sharing between the military and those political forces willing and able to engage it.

Now, with Mubarak out of power, the Brotherhood entered the fray in earnest; and from the moment it mobilized, it advanced a democratic agenda. Yusuf al-Qaradawi, the most senior cleric associated with the Brotherhood, returned to Egypt after years in exile and addressed more than a million people in an open-air Friday sermon on February 18. Instead of beginning with the interpellation "O Muslims!," Qaradawi opted for a more inclusive address: "O Muslims and Copts!" He then went on to reiterate the argument for the perfect compatibility of Islam and democracy that he had expressed in his articles and books while in exile. The symbolic weight of the moment was broadly felt. Here, in his first opportunity to address free Egyptians, the man who more than any other provided an ideological justification for the contemporary Brotherhood was choosing to speak about democratic values as a link to faith.

The degree of public support for Islamic democratic values was determined in the first instance by rolling parliamentary elections that took place from November 2011 to January 2012. The results were fully consistent with the hypothesis that Islamic democrats would prevail in any fair election in the Arabic-speaking world. The party associated with the Muslim Brotherhood took 45 percent of the seats. In a surprisingly strong finish, another Islamic democratic party, Al-Nour, took a quarter of the available seats. This latter party, referred to popularly as the salafis, took public positions that were religiously to the right of the Brotherhood, calling in a rather nonspecific way for still greater influence for shari'a in political governance. But the salafis were nonetheless democratic in their orientation: they embraced elections as legitimate and desirable, and were willing to express public commitment to the equality of all Egyptians, regardless of religion. Their success came largely from their capacity to appeal to poorer Egyptians who saw the Brotherhood as a middle-class movement. The moment they found themselves in possession of the political power of which they had dreamed for generations, the Islamists of the Brotherhood found themselves faced with a serious challenge: dealing with a military that showed no great haste to relinquish its power. From one perspective, the Brotherhood and the military were at odds. After all, the Brotherhood had advocated democracy, and had now been vindicated by public support. The military's role was decidedly undemocratic. The SCAF had ordered the drafting of constitutional reforms and gotten them approved by the public long before it allowed the parliamentary elections. It maintained a watchful eye over the executive functions previously exercised by the president. Presidential elections would not be held until much later in 2012—and even then, many observers anticipated a relatively weak president who would remain beholden to the military to get things done.

From another perspective, however, the interests of the Brotherhood and the military were aligned. The political class newly elected to office understood that the military remained a crucial locus of power in an Egyptian society facing rapid and uncertain transition. Not only in the realm of self-defense but in the realm of maintaining domestic order, the military was a necessary partner for any effective government. What was more, the military had close ties to the government of the United States, Egypt's primary source of foreign aid. The continued presence of the military as a public force in Egyptian life served as an assurance to its American allies that things in Egypt had not changed so much that the U.S.-Egyptian relationship had to be rethought.

In particular, the Brotherhood needed some visible public signal to communicate to the United States its seriousness about respecting the Camp David accords and maintaining the cold peace that obtained between Egypt and Israel in the Mubarak years. Many American government officials feared that a government dominated by the Brotherhood would change the status quo and revoke the peace treaty that President Anwar Sadat signed with Israel in 1978. After all, the peace treaty had always been unpopular in Egypt, and the stance of the Muslim Brotherhood toward Israel was expected to be hostile at best. The leverage that the United States enjoyed vis-à-vis Egypt depended upon the more than $1.3 billion in annual aid, mostly military, that it had sent without fail to Egypt since the treaty was signed. Any significant change in Egypt's public position with respect to Israel was likely to lead Congress to rethink that aid—and fast.

The Egyptian military, the prime beneficiary of that aid, had developed strong institutional ties with the U.S. military during the period since Camp David. There was little doubt that the military would want the treaty to remain in place in order to avoid losing the financial and institutional links that enabled it to remain strong and effective. To the extent that the Muslim Brotherhood also wanted to avoid rocking the boat in the Egypt-U.S. relationship, the Brotherhood had a strong incentive to keep the military as part of the power structure.

Strikingly, the Brotherhood did appear committed to preserving a close relationship with the United States. As a matter of foreign policy, this position was wholly rational. In the post–Cold War environment, Egypt had no stronger potential regional ally. Russia was no longer a major player in the Middle East, and China had not yet begun to take an active role except in countries with significant oil reserves, which Egypt lacks. Especially given the strong and continuing U.S. support of Israel, Egypt's medium-term national self-interest called for continued closeness to the United States.

But what was more remarkable is that the Brotherhood's Islamist politics did not prove a barrier to continuing to respect international treaties that Egypt had signed—including the peace treaty with Israel. This remains true despite the fact that Hamas, the Palestinian offshoot of the Muslim Brotherhood, traditionally took a hard line toward Israel in comparison with the Palestine Liberation Organization, or Fatah. When it comes to Israel policy, Islamic democrats will continue to face a subtle set of choices. They must, if they wish to serve the interests of their countries, pursue a rational foreign policy that takes into account the power of the United States. At the same time, to a much greater extent than the dictators who governed in the region, they must pay attention to public opinion if they want to get reelected.

In 2003 I argued (somewhat unpopularly, it must be admitted) that Islamic democrats would not be ineluctably anti-Israel. Indeed, I claimed that "over time, democracy in the Arab world should actually make lasting peace with Israel more likely." This view depended on the proposition that Islamic democrats would not have to rely on anti-Israel sentiments to gain popular legitimacy in the way that some regional dictators did for many years. Naturally, there is strong pro-Palestinian sentiment among ordinary voters in the Arabic-speaking world. But this sympathy should logically result in support for a negotiated peace between Israel and Palestine. Such a peace would be much more likely to be perceived as legitimate if negotiated by elected Palestinian leaders and supported by elected Arab governments.

It is still too soon to see if this analysis will prove correct. However, it is encouraging that not only the Muslim Brotherhood but even the salafis, positioned to their right, have sought to convey the impression that they will respect Camp David. If the Brotherhood can lead a government that recognizes Israel and deals with it, there is reason to hope that Hamas, historically linked to the Brotherhood and derived from it, might move in the same direction. Certainly a Brotherhood in political power in Egypt exercises greater influence over Hamas than any other regional power might. In February 2012, Hamas political leader Ismail Haniya took the opportunity of a speech at Al-Azhar in Cairo to express solidarity with the uprising against Syrian dictator Bashar al-Assad. This was an extraordinary development given that Hamas had been headquartered in Syria for many years and had routinely received support from Assad's backers in Iran. To break with one's patrons in this public way was a marker of realignment by Hamas, from Syria to Egypt. Although one could plausibly construe this development as threatening to the prospects of peace, this does not seem to be the most convincing interpretation. If Hamas is aligned with a government that is at peace with Israel, the likelihood of a peaceful resolution is much greater than when Hamas is aligned with two governments implacably opposed to its interests.

⚭

The complex relationship between the Muslim Brotherhood and the Egyptian military raises the all-important question of how power will be balanced in the new Egyptian Islamic state— a question I take up in the last part of this book. The challenge lies in establishing institutions with the capacity to balance one another in order to ensure that the rule of law can function. The aspiration to govern according to the principles of shari'a will provide cultural support for the ideal of the rule of law. But even well-meaning governments fail if the constitutional arrangements within them do not create the proper incentives to balance power.

Ideally, in the modern constitutional state, the balance involves legislative, executive, and judicial authorities. These need not be formally separate for the balance to work. In parliamentary systems, executive power is typically exercised by a prime minister who is not in any sense independent of the legislature, with the help of a cabinet presiding over professionalized ministries. The point is, however, that whether the system is parliamentary, presidential, or some combination of these, the balance is achieved among civilian authorities.

Yet there are examples, both historical and more recent, of constitutional balance that involves the military, whether for a long duration or during some period of extended transition. In the Ottoman Empire, dealt with extensively in the first part of the book, the janissary corps had a significant constitutional role alongside the scholars and the sultan. In modern Turkey, the army for decades adopted a constitutional role as guarantor of secularism—a role from which it seems now to be retreating.

Can the Egyptian army play a similar balancing role, to the advantage of the Islamic democrats of the Brotherhood? If it does, will the military accept a gradual retreat from exercising de facto constitutional power if and when democratic institutions begin to flourish on their own? In general, the track record of militaries claiming to intervene selectively in democratic politics is not good. The Algerian military, which reversed the results of the 1991 elections there, conducted a long and bloody civil war against the Islamists. When it had won, it kept itself in power and maintained dictatorial control. The reason that the Arab Spring never reached Algeria—and shows little inclination to do so in the future—had everything to do with the overwhelming power of the military in the wake of its victory in the civil war there. Unlike Tunisia and Egypt, where the military ultimately chose not to support the regime in the face of popular protests, in Algeria there was no meaningful difference between the military and the regime at all.

Yet it is just possible that the Egyptian military might successfully negotiate a medium-term deal with the Brotherhood that would actually help constitutional balance. The Brotherhood initially hoped not to run a candidate for the presidency in the spring of 2012, thus assuring that any elected president would be relatively weak, since he would not be from the party that held nearly half the seats in the legislature. This initial strategy—which had to be abandoned when a dissident former Brotherhood leader announced his candidacy and began to poll well—represented a substantial concession to the military. It looked like a promise by the Brotherhood not to challenge the military for total power in the early years of the new state. In turn, the Brotherhood hoped to reserve the right to criticize the military, to protest against it if its policies seemed insufficiently democratic—and above all to blame it for future problems that Egypt was sure to face in the years ahead. This strategic restraint on the part of the Brotherhood suggested a fairly high degree of sophistication about the need to establish constitutional balance over a course of several years. But with the Brotherhood ultimately deciding to field a candidate, and the results of the election unknown as of this writing, the way that balance will develop remains seriously in doubt.

Over the longer term, achieving constitutional balance among civilians will require a sophisticated development of civilian institutions. This the Islamic democrats will have to undertake experimentally. In the case of Egypt, the constitution does not need to be amended to make shari'a into a source of law—it already does so. Nor would the constitution have to be amended in order to create Islamic judicial review. The Egyptian constitutional court already has the responsibility of determining that the provisions of the constitution, including those involving Islam, are followed. Over time, the Brotherhood might want to enact legislation that more closely corresponds to shariʿa than laws passed by the rubber-stamp legislature under dictatorship. The Brotherhood might also eventually wish to alter the composition of the constitutional court to include judges trained in shariʿa, not only secular law. But these possible future developments have not been emphasized thus far in the Brotherhood's public statements. To the contrary, the Brotherhood seems focused on managing the military and establishing effective electoral democracy.

⨝

In other areas where the Arab Spring brought changes, the future is still more uncertain. In Libya, a regionally focused popular uprising was met with military force by Muammar Qaddafi. But Qaddafi overplayed his hand in threatening to hunt down and kill the rebels. Expressing concern for the threat of a humanitarian disaster that had not yet fully come to pass, France, Britain, and the United States got a UN Security Council resolution authorizing force to protect civilians. NATO then undertook an air war aimed at removing Qaddafi from power in concert with rebel forces. Over the course of several months, the strategy eventually succeeded, and Qaddafi was killed by the rebels.

This abrupt transition left Libya in a rather ambiguous state. Rebel forces were not sufficiently organized to form an immediately effective government. Militias had been divided along both regional and tribal lines, conditions making the emergence of a unified government extremely challenging. As the example of Iraq shows, when an extended bombing campaign destroys the infrastructure of the dictatorial state, a significant period of disorder can result before something like real government emerges. And this was true even under conditions of U.S. occupation. In Libya, the absence of an occupying force may help forestall civil war; but it also means that there is no single entity with the capacity to subdue the country. The rebels, after all, did not win the war on their own, and could not have done so. Their ultimate success depended on foreign air power, which they cannot deploy to maintain law and order. Elections have not yet occurred as of this writing. A substantial Islamist component surfaced during the rebellion, but whether it will follow the Islamic democratic tendencies of Tunisia and Egypt remains to be seen.

Yemen is a particularly complex and challenging case. Like Ben Ali, Mubarak, and Qaddafi, its president, Ali Abdullah Saleh, was aging and facing a transition after his thirty-three years in power. Resistance to his regime emerged during the early months of 2011, initially involving protests of approximately twenty thousand people in the chief cities of San'a and 'Aden. An important organizer of some of these protests was Tawakel Karman, a young Yemeni activist who would soon be awarded the 2011 Nobel Peace Prize for her role. Karman belongs to the Islah Party, which is connected to the Yemeni branch of the Muslim Brotherhood—but is also the political vehicle of the Ahmar clan, Saleh's chief tribal opponent. Karman's role and her political affiliation made Yemen's democratic uprising resemble the aftermath of the other Arab Spring protests, marked by the involvement of Islamic democrats like Karman.

Faced with these protests, Saleh wavered. In May 2011 he was injured when a bomb went off in his presidential palace. Leaving the country, he continued to assert authority. Eventually, under pressure from allies in the Gulf, Saleh agreed to transfer power to his longtime vice president, Abd Rabbuh Mansur Al-Hadi, who was then elected nearly unanimously in

February 2012. Hadi promised to preside over the drafting of a new constitution and to step down after two years in office. Whether he keeps these promises remains to be seen.

Election results in Yemen are likely to be quite different from those in Tunisia and Egypt. In largely rural Yemen, tribal politics matter as much as or more than slogans of Islamic democracy. Throughout the period of the uprising, Saleh and his supporters strove to depict what was happening as a power grab by the Ahmar clan—and so it sometimes appeared. To make matters more complicated, in some parts of Yemen the government's writ does not run—nor has it ever. The Yemeni state today probably lacks a monopoly on the use of legitimate violence in a significant portion of the country, and that has always been the case. Nevertheless, Yemen is poised on the edge of greater democracy and constitutional reform; these are likely to take an at least superficially Islamist direction.

This leaves Syria as the last of the countries where the events and energies unleashed by the Arab Spring remain seriously unresolved. The protest movement in Syria began much more slowly than did the protests in the other countries where they took on major significance. And when peaceful demonstrations began to take off in Syria, they did not occur in the major population centers of Damascus and Aleppo. Instead they happened in smaller, Sunni-dominated cities at the periphery, most importantly Dar'a, on the Jordanian border, and Homs, Syria's third-largest city.

The reason for the locations was important. The Assad regime is based upon the denominational solidarity of the 'Alawi religious community in Syria, which makes up perhaps 12 percent of the population. Hafez Al-Assad, the progenitor of the regime, initially came to power via the Syrian branch of the Ba'th Party, a secular Arab nationalist movement that sought to transcend religious or denominational difference. Michel

Aflaq, the leading ideologue of Ba'thism, was a Christian; and of course there was nothing wrong with the goal of inclusion. But Ba'thist ideology rather quickly evolved to provide cover for oppressive, dictatorial regimes in Iraq and Syria. In the latter case, it afforded a rubric for a regime that selects both senior government officials and, more importantly, senior military leaders based upon 'Alawi identity.

In what was effectively a minority regime, the government was long able to command the loyalty of 'Alawis by warning of the retribution that would be taken by the majority Sunni community should power be lost. An effective state security apparatus was able to control political affairs in much of the country even after the protests began. The absence of protests in Damascus and Aleppo was taken as evidence of the regime's legitimacy among an urban middle class and of the effective power of the security apparatus in maintaining the regime's control. By contrast, the emergence of protests at the periphery suggested the possibility of gradual erosion of that control.

When the protests did not subside, the Assad regime responded with aggressive military force, eventually including ground and air assaults as well as shelling. This path, not taken by the armies of Tunisia and Egypt, followed that of Qaddafi— but with an important difference. Where Qaddafi had no international constituency at all, Assad was the beneficiary of support from three different quarters.

First was Iran, the main backer of the Assad regime since the collapse of the Soviet Union. Iran stood to lose substantially if Assad were to fall. As a militant, non-Arab, and Shi'i state, the Islamic Republic of Iran had never found a stable ally among the predominantly Sunni Arab states until it was able to cobble together a relationship with Syria's 'Alawis. (Although 'Alawism is in some sense a branch of Shi'ism, theology is not the basis for the relationship; what matters more is that the Assad regime depended upon repressing Sunni political aspirations within Syria.) Iran has also relied upon Syria as a geographical avenue to support Lebanese Hezbollah, the Shi'i militia-cum-political party that is Iran's most direct foreign-policy tool with regard to Israel.

Besides Iran, Syria enjoyed an ongoing relationship with Russia under President, then Prime Minister, then again President, Vladimir Putin. A veteran of the KGB's Middle East service, Putin was an Arabic speaker whose intelligence career coincided with the era of staunch Soviet support for Syria. Although the constraints of limited resources in a post-Soviet world meant that Putin's influence in Syria could not approach that of his Soviet predecessors, he nevertheless maintained strong diplomatic support of Syria—now Russia's only meaningful ally in the U.S.-dominated region. Most crucially for Assad, with Russian support came a veto in the Security Council. When Britain, France, and the United States sought Security Council permission to bomb Libya, Russia and China abstained, partly because they had no close ties to Qaddafi and partly because they may have reasonably imagined that, after the failures of Iraq, these allies would not seek to achieve regime change from the air in the Middle East. When Security Council resolutions were sought to condemn Assad, Russia exercised its veto. It had no desire to be used once more to provide cover for regime change that would remove an ally.

A more surprising ally for Syria in its struggle against international condemnation of its increasingly violent efforts to suppress its democracy movement was China, not historically a close ally of the regime. China's interest lay mostly in avoiding the precedent of Western democratic powers intervening by force to support democratic protests against autocracy. Beyond this was China's looming geostrategic rise relative to the United States. Put simply, the fall of the Assad regime would harm Iran and help the United States, underscoring America's position as the dominant regional power. Such a gain for the United States would not serve China's interest in gradually eroding U.S. world dominance. Taken in whatever proportion, these motivations were enough to get China to join Russia in vetoing a resolution that might have facilitated external support for Syria's democracy movement.

Freed from the immediate threat of international intervention, Assad's forces proved able to make significant progress in suppressing protests. Gradually, and in response, peaceful demonstrations began to give way to violence against Syrian troops and government targets by emergent Sunni militias. Whether sticking with nonviolent resistance would have been a superior strategy was beside the point. The conflict began inexorably to take on the flavor of a violent insurrection or low-level civil war.

As they had done in Libya, protesters with militiamen at their sides gradually "liberated" parts of the country. The most significant locale to fall into the protesters' hands was Homs, a city of eight hundred thousand and the site of some of the most important early protests. Once again, Assad's reaction was brutal and effective. In February and March 2012, the Syrian military shelled Homs and drove protesters and militias from the city.

It remains to be seen whether this classic tactic of counterinsurgency could be repeated until the uprising was completely suppressed. Some close observers had come to believe that the regime's days were inevitably numbered, and that the trends of the Arab Spring were against it. Others believed that Bashar Al-Assad, the only young dictator challenged during the Arab Spring, stood a reasonable chance of successfully restoring power. Assad himself seems to have believed either that he was likely to succeed or, alternatively, that with apparent war crimes on his hands, he had no other option but to fight on. Syria's military suffered some desertions of enlisted soldiers, but there was no outwardly visible sign of unrest among the officer corps, whether senior or junior. Doubtless the reason had much to do with successful regime efforts to keep that corps overwhelmingly 'Alawi.

What is the meaning of the violent turn that the Arab Spring has taken in Syria for the future of Islamic democracy there or elsewhere? The first lesson is that coming to power through peaceful protests is far from inevitable, even where public support is quite broad. Where the military sticks close to the regime, even large and persistent public protests will not suffice to bring about revolutionary change. The military was crucial in ending the dictatorships of Ben Ali and Mubarak, and Qaddafi could not have fallen without external military force.

Second, even peaceful protest can veer into violence when the provocation is sufficiently great. This was true in Libya and has proven true in Syria as well. Protesters may begin by assuming, correctly, that the international community will be more sympathetic to them if their strategy is nonviolent resistance. But when family members are being killed, and the authority of the state is in question, there is a great temptation to undertake armed resistance—even when the odds of success seem slim. It is also possible that Syrian Sunnis who took up arms were looking at the model of international intervention in Libya. Their expectation that the regime would use force against civilians was satisfied. What has not come to pass—at least not as of this writing—is for the international community to respond with any actual use of force to what have repeatedly been called crimes against humanity. Russian and Chinese support for the regime will make it far harder for any coordinated international response to take place against Assad. If the Sunni militias were at all inspired by the possibility of being helped like their Libyan counterparts, they must so far have been sorely disappointed.

The third lesson of the Syrian uprising for Islamist politics is that violence creates conditions favorable to jihadism rather than democratically oriented Islamism. Iraq had already provided ample evidence to this effect, as Islamist militias of both Sunni and Shi'a stripes made it much harder for Islamic democrats to establish their legitimacy. Only the defeat of those militias opened a door for the normalization of Islamic democratic politics. Should the Iraqi state again be seriously challenged by a Sunni insurgency, one could expect radical jihadis to participate once more.

The contrast between the Islamic democrats of Tunisia and Egypt and the budding militias in Syria is equally stark. There have been persistent rumors of al-Qaeda participation in those militias—rumors that could plausibly be true, inasmuch as al-Qaeda did infiltrate Sunni militias in Iraq. When fighting a war, one tends to be less picky about one's allies than one would be in peacetime. And al-Qaeda's ideological commitment to the idea that only force can prevail finds a natural breeding ground in a time and place where democratic politics seem to have failed.

⌘

Should Syria's troubles be resolved by some democratic solution that removes Assad from power, only Algeria and Sudan would remain of the major dictatorial regimes of the Arab world. This would represent a radical transformation of regional politics and a decisive step in the direction of the rise of the Islamic state. It can hardly be doubted that a democratic government that managed to emerge in Syria after Assad would be Islamist in its orientation. One can only hope that it would also be democratic; but the influence of the other Islamic democrats in the region is reason to consider that the more likely outcome if Assad should fall.

Yet one fascinating aspect of the Arab Spring has been the list of Arab countries where its effects have been felt only obliquely—a list that consists overwhelmingly of the region's monarchies. Not a single monarchy has fallen in the Arab Spring. Not a single monarchy has seen its legitimacy significantly shaken by mass protests. The reasons for this shed light on the question of Islam, constitutional democracy, and the balance of power.

The two Arab monarchies where the Arab Spring had perhaps the greatest effects without fundamentally challenging legitimacy were the two countries where young kings had already been delivering gradual, if limited, constitutional reforms: Morocco and Jordan. In both places, the kings were veterans of the struggle to maintain legitimacy through co-optation rather than coercion alone. Both monarchs reacted to the Arab Spring by speeding up reform processes that already existed. In both cases, this meant an expanded role for Islamic democrats.

In Morocco, for the first time, Mohammed VI allowed the party affiliated with the local Muslim Brotherhood to form a government—a result that would have been unthinkable just a few years before. He also introduced constitutional reforms that would modestly expand political freedom while preserving the preeminent position of the *makhzen*, or royal state apparatus. In essence, Mohammed's response was to acknowledge that the result of the increased freedom created by the Arab Spring was increased success for Islamic democrats. By allowing the Brotherhood to govern, he was opting for the result without opening the process. The move seems to have worked. Protests in Morocco abated, and the legitimacy of the monarchy does not seem to have been shaken.

In Jordan, King 'Abdullah trod more carefully—and his options were fewer. It was already true that the only really important political party in the country was the one associated with the Brotherhood. In response to early 2011 protests, in which the Brotherhood participated, 'Abdullah dismissed his prime minister and cabinet and appointed new ones. He also promised to speed political reform. Protests abated slightly but never fully stopped. Later in 2011, the new prime minister resigned in response to continuing protests.

'Abdullah's gamble seems to be that, over time, protests will die down as the spirit of the Arab Spring subsides. His responsiveness to protest mirrors his historical practice of trying to accommodate Islamic democratic impulses in the population without transferring real power. That strategy worked before the Arab Spring, and there is every reason to expect it will continue to work afterward. Meanwhile, the violence in Syria serves as a reminder to Jordanians that disorder can follow a change in the existing regime.

The relative successes of Mohammed and Abdullah in managing the Arab Spring suggest not only that young leaders have an advantage over older ones in responding to protests, but also that, in the Arabic-speaking world today, monarchy may actually function as a more legitimate type of government than dictatorship. Part of the reason is duration: the Moroccan monarchy can claim to be generations old, and 'Abdullah is the third long-serving Hashemite king in a dynasty that has endured for nearly a century. Monarchies also manage transitions better than dictatorships, because the idea of succession is already implicit in the monarchic structure. Each king inherited his job from a father who died of old age. But unlike Bashar Al-Assad, who also inherited his position when his father died, or Gamal Mubarak, expected by many observers to succeed his father, the kings could claim that this inheritance was their lawful right.

But probably more significant than these factors was that the kings of Morocco and Jordan always derived their legitimacy from something beyond simple fear. Relative to the region's dictatorships, these two monarchies had always deployed sophisticated strategies to legitimate their rule, ranging from religion in Morocco to tribal ties in Jordan to complex and ramified royal patronage in both places. As part of this quest for legitimacy, each had been willing to offer partially legitimate democratic institutions in which Islamic democrats were already participating. Under these circumstances, public unrest may have been just as persistent and powerful as it was in the dictatorships. But it did not represent as radical a change in political norms. Put another way, these quasi-constitutional monarchs had *already* accommodated would-be Islamic democrats much more than the dictators had done. They could therefore continue to do so without allowing for revolutionary change to occur.

In the oil monarchies, the situation was different yet again. Bahrain underwent the most significant protests, driven by a mostly Shiʻi population that had grown restive under the Sunni monarchy. Initial protests did not directly challenge the monarchy's right to rule, but as the monarchy responded by violently clearing protesters and killing several, the themes and slogans changed.

Alarmed by the turn the protests were taking, King Hamad turned to extreme measures. On March 14, 2011, a thousand Saudi troops crossed the causeway into Bahrain in support of the monarchy. Alongside five hundred well-armed police borrowed from the United Arab Emirates, they engaged in a show of force in support of Bahraini police and troops who put down the main protests. The fight took several days. Several demonstrators were killed and hundreds were arrested. The message from the monarchy—and from neighboring Saudi Arabia—could not have been clearer: the Arab Spring would not be permitted to challenge the power of the kings in the Gulf. Their legitimacy, such as it was, would be backed by overwhelming force.

In this, as in every aspect of political or constitutional life in the Gulf, oil played a predominant role. The nearly unlimited coffers of Saudi Arabia function as a force field that distorts ordinary rules of political economy. Bahrain has relatively little by way of oil and natural gas. But its proximity to Saudi Arabia meant that what happened there might have a demonstration effect for Saudi Arabia; and that provided the Saudi impetus to intervene. Much of Saudi Arabia's oil wealth is found in the Shi'i-majority eastern province. The Saudi royal family had no interest in allowing Bahrain's Shi'is to make a play for power that could inspire Shi'is across the border. There have, in fact, been small, continuing Shi'i protests in Saudi Arabia. All have been met with arrests and massive shows of force.

It is unclear what electoral results would follow if any of the Gulf monarchies were pushed aside. Islamic democratic politics have been deployed by domestic dissidents in several states as a form of protest. In Saudi Arabia, where the scholars have legitimated the monarchy in a distinctive, oil-fueled version of the traditional Sunni constitutional arrangement, it is unclear how much support for democracy might potentially exist. One is inclined to doubt that any such support would run deep. Islamic democratic politics have in general been most effective when used against secular regimes, not regimes that make plausible claims to Islamic legitimacy. But in any event, the issue is purely hypothetical for the foreseeable future. The oil monarchies of the Gulf survived the Arab Spring more or less unscathed.

What emerges from the foregoing account is, I think, a series of rather concrete proofs for some of the arguments of the book you hold in your hands. First, the claim that the call for shariʿa is a call for the rule of law expressed through constitutional democracy: this is precisely the program of the Islamic democrats who have been elected in the wake of regime change in Tunisia and Egypt. Second, the claim that dictatorial governments in the Arabic-speaking world were characterized by a fundamental imbalance of power: such dictatorships are now noticeably on the decline, but their features persist in those regimes, like the Assad regime in Syria, where the old norms prevail. Third, the institutional challenges that will be faced by Islamic democrats when they do in fact get the opportunity to shape the new Islamic states: the challenges of both democratizing and constitutionalizing the shariʿa are now being addressed by constitutional reformers in Tunisia and Egypt.

This book ends on a note of caution, not triumphalism. The aspiration to craft Islamic constitutional democracy is no guarantee that the effort will be successful. The underlying historical argument of this book is that classical Islamic constitutionalism, in its many variants, worked because it entailed the balance of power between the scholars who declared and interpreted the law and the rulers who implemented it and exercised executive authority. When that balance shifted, the system failed to restore the balance in a new way. Most of the governments that followed also failed to meet the requirements of balance, with predictably poor results for political governance.

The new Islamic states will succeed if, and only if, they develop institutional capacities that will allow them to establish new forms of balance and enable the rule of law to function. The Arab Spring means that more countries will have the opportunity to try. The test cases will not be restricted to strange circumstances of occupation and state collapse like those in Afghanistan and Iraq. Democratic revolution from within will be given a chance to operate. In Tunisia and Egypt, at least, Islamic democrats have the opportunity to operate outside the constraints and distractions of resistance to unjust powers, whether colonial or domestic. We are at a historic crossroads with respect to the rise of the Islamic state. The direction that state follows will be fascinating and important—and it will be revealed in the years ahead.

INTRODUCTION

WHEN EMPIRES FALL, they tend to stay dead. The same is true of government systems. Monarchy has been in steady decline since the American Revolution, and today it is hard to imagine a resurgence of royalty anywhere in the world. The fall of the Soviet bloc dealt a deathblow to communism; now no one expects Marx to make a comeback. Even China's ruling party is communist only in name.

There are, however, two prominent examples of governing systems reemerging after they had apparently ceased to exist. One is democracy, a form of government that had some limited success in a small Greek city-state for a couple of hundred years, disappeared, and then was resurrected some two thousand years later. Its re-creators were non-Greeks, living under radically different conditions, for whom democracy was a word handed down in the philosophy books, to be embraced only fitfully and after some serious reinterpretation. The other is the Islamic state.

From the time the Prophet Muhammad and his followers withdrew from Mecca to form their own political community until just after World War I—almost exactly thirteen hundred years—Islamic governments ruled states that ranged from fortified towns to transcontinental empires. These states, separated in time, space, and size, were so Islamic that they did not need the adjective to describe themselves. A common constitutional theory, developing and changing over the course of cen-

1

turies, obtained in all. A Muslim ruler governed according to God's law, expressed through principles and rules of the shari'a that were expounded by scholars. The ruler's fulfillment of the duty to command what the law required and ban what it prohibited made his authority lawful and legitimate.

In the nineteenth century, distinctively Islamic government began to falter. The Ottoman Empire, whose ruler claimed to lead the Islamic world as caliph, adopted a series of new governing arrangements championed by internal reformers and pressed by Western debt-holders. Though the empire remained formally Islamic, epochal changes like a legislature and a legislative code shook the foundations of the traditional, unwritten constitution that had prevailed under traditional Islamic rule. When the Ottoman Empire collapsed in the wake of its defeat in World War I, its lands were divided into Western spheres of influence, guided, if not governed, by France and England. The new Turkish government that eventually established itself on the Ottoman Empire's Anatolian rump declared itself secular and abolished the caliphate. In both symbolic and practical terms, the Islamic state died in 1924.

Yet today the Islamic state rides again. Its reach is not limited to fascinating anomalies like Saudi Arabia, which claims to adhere to the ancient Islamic constitution in its purest form. By revolution, as in Iran, or by constitutional referendum, as in Iraq and Afghanistan, governments in majority-Muslim countries are increasingly declaring themselves Islamic. Their new constitutional regimes replace secular arrangements adopted over the last century with government based in some way on the shari'a. The trend is with them. In Muslim countries running the geographical span from Morocco to Indonesia, substantial majorities say that the shari'a should be a source of law for their states; and in important and populous countries like Egypt and Pakistan, large majorities say that Islamic law should be the *only* source of legislation.[1] Wherever democratic elections are held in Muslim countries, large numbers of citizens vote for shari'a-oriented political parties that are best characterized as Islamist. The programs of these parties differ little from place to place. They embrace democratic elections and basic rights. They promise economic reform, an end to corruption, and above all, the adoption of the shari'a as a source or the source of law.[2]

This movement toward the Islamic state is riding a wave of nostalgia, but it is also looking forward. The designers and advocates of the new Islamic state want to recapture the core of what made the traditional Islamic state great. They declare their allegiance to the shari'a, while simultaneously announcing an affinity for democracy.[3] This means that the new Islamic state will be different from the old one. There is no turning back the clock of history, no matter what anyone says.

The Islamists' aims are both religious and worldly. To be sure, they seek to follow God's will. But they also explicitly say that they want to restore just government and world significance to the countries in which they live. Without these stated goals—and the chance that it might be possible to accomplish them—the Islamists would have little or no popular support. Political actors in the contemporary Muslim world, from ordinary voters to elites, take Islam seriously as a basis for government only to the extent that they believe it can make a practical difference in places where both the state and society itself have fallen on hard times.

Can the new Islamic state succeed? This question has enormous implications for the residents of Muslim countries and for the rest of the world that must engage with Islamic states and movements that promote Islam as a political solution. To answer it requires getting behind the slogans that characterize both sides of the debate. In the first place, we must get a clearer sense of what the traditional Islamic state actually was, and why it worked so well for so many centuries until it ultimately declined and fell. Only then will we see fully why the idea of the Islamic state is so popular today. We will also then be able to figure out whether the new Islamic state might be able to recapture some relevant features of the old state that would make it work. Most important, we will be able to identify the major challenges that will face the new Islamic states—challenges that will shape their behavior toward their own citizens and toward the rest of the world.

Toward a New Interpretation of Islamic Constitutional History

The fall of the Islamic state and its unlikely rebirth form the topic of this book. My purpose, though, is not only historical. I want to propose an interpretation of the Islamic constitution in its old and new forms that will help clarify where we are today and where we are going with respect to government in the Muslim world. The future of the Islamic state is very much under formation—but so is its past, which is not really over so long as its meaning is being debated and its outcome remains undetermined.

In this sense, my approach takes seriously the arguments of those Muslims who are trying to reconstruct an Islamic state that will succeed in the face of contemporary conditions. For them, the past of the Islamic state is not some dead hand but the living, breathing material from which the future will be built. The medieval scholars whose ideas I will have occasion to discuss are as good as alive, and their writings and lives provide guidance for action.

There is nothing unique to Muslims about this active and continuing engagement with the constitutional past. Madison, Jefferson, and Hamilton continue to shape the American constitutional tradition from beyond the grave. It is impossible to understand arguments about the American Constitution today without taking these founding fathers into account, and no one would maintain that this makes constitutional debate in the United States premodern. Yet much analysis of the Muslim world insists on an artificial distinction between the historical past, the preserve of a professional guild of historians, and forward-looking political analysis, itself divided between university political scientists and think tank or government analysts.

To be sure, the collapse of the traditional Islamic state is part of the reason for the divide between history and the present in thinking about the constitutional structure of the Muslim world. This rupture with the past, a break sometimes rather portentously called "modernity," undeniably did take place. The caliphate really was abolished. As we shall see, the shar'ia lost its formal preeminence, and the scholars who were the keepers of the law were correspondingly demoted and displaced. The new states that replaced the old proclaimed their discontinuity with their predecessors.

All these events will play a central role in our story of fall and rise. But accepting the historical law that dead empires do not rise again may lead us to miss what is probably the single most important aspect of the new Islamic state, namely, its aspiration to reclaim the glories of the old one. An account of how the new Islamic state will fare in its struggle to achieve this aspiration has to transcend the divide between past and present, just like the Islamic state as conceived by its proponents.

I begin in Part I by asking why the idea of the Islamic state looks so attractive today to people whose own grandparents rejected such a state as a relic of the failed past. Of course the call for a return to the shari'a is complex, shaped by factors including the failure of secular autocracy, the appeal of socially conservative religion in an uncertain world, and the yearning for spiritual revitalization. The very word "shari'a" conjures images of social control through severe criminal punishment and the regulation of sexual morality, especially that of women. Some advocates of the shari'a are no doubt motivated by the desire to achieve such goals. But what is less often noticed is the basic fact that the ideal of the shari'a invokes the core idea of law in terms that resonate deeply with the Islamic past. The Islamic state is preeminently a shari'a state, defined by its commitment to a vision of legal order.[4] The state historically organized under what I shall call the classical or the traditional Islamic constitution—a constitution that, like the English constitution, was unwritten and ever-evolving—was a *legal* state in both meanings of the term.[5] The system was justified *by* law, and the system administered basic government *through* law.[6]

Both elements of this constitutional structure depended crucially on a balance between the authority of the ruler and the law itself. But the law was no abstraction. It was analyzed, discussed, applied, discovered, and (an outsider would say) made by the members of a distinct social-political grouping known as the scholars, or in Arabic *'ulama*. From this scholarly class came not only theologians and other intellectuals but the appointed judges who decided concrete cases and independent jurists who opined as to the meaning of the law. Through their near monopoly on legal affairs in a state where God's law was accepted as paramount, the scholars—especially those of them who focused on law[7]—built themselves into a powerful and effective check on the ruler. To see the Islamic constitution as containing the balance of powers so necessary for a functioning, sustainable legal state is to emphasize not why it failed, as all forms of government eventually must, but why it succeeded so spectacularly for as long as it did.

In Part II, I give my own reasons for the collapse of this old order. The source of the collapse, I suggest, was not only the very real crisis that faced the Ottoman Empire in the mid-nineteenth century when it realized that Western states were beginning, for the first time, to outpace their Eastern counterparts in state building. That crisis certainly called for a response; and the Ottoman reformers who ushered in the period of change known as the Tanzimat were on the right track in thinking that political liberalization and fiscal responsibility would improve the economic state of the empire and thus rescue it from second-class status.

The key to the disaster was the incomplete manner in which the Ottoman reforms were adopted. The single most durable feature of the reforms turned out to be the removal of effective lawmaking authority from the scholars through the substitution of written legal codes for the common law of the shari'a. Around the same time, a constitution was promulgated creating a legislature. The legal authority of the constitution could potentially have substituted for the role classically played by the shari'a in ordaining the rule of law. The legislature could have functioned as an institutional check on the authority of the ruler, and thereby substituted for the historic role of the scholars in keeping the ruler's executive authority in check. But the constitution and legislature were effectively retracted and abolished by Sultan Abdulhamid II. That left behind the legal codes, eventually reconceived as state law emanating from the sovereign, not the preserve of scholars independently interpreting God's will.

With no constitution and no legislature, and with the scholars removed from control over the law, no check whatever remained on the authority of the sultan.[8] Earlier Islamic dynasties had been replaced by later ones without destroying the form of the Islamic state; but the half-accomplished Ottoman reforms sank the whole system. When the Ottoman Empire was defeated in World War I, the governments that replaced it—including those under Western colonial influence—preserved the essential function of the Ottoman law codes and the late-Ottoman innovation of relegating the scholars to the role of minor religious functionaries. Outside the former empire's domains, a similar tendency toward codification often managed to displace the scholarly class from its traditional role in shaping the legal order, with similar results. The scholars and their shari'a never again regained their lost status as the legitimating source of constitutional authority. The constitution of the classical Islamic state had passed from the scene.

In the light of this account of the fall of the Islamic state, I then go on in Part II to discuss the distinctive limitations and pathologies of the modern states that arose to replace it in the Muslim world. The governments of these states have proved to be surprisingly skilled at preserving political order within specified borders. They have been disastrously bad, however, at creating conditions that would make them seem morally legitimate to their own citizens. For that they would have to deliver basic political justice: the sense among ordinary people that the system treats them as they deserve to be treated, not depriving them of opportunities available to other peoples elsewhere or of their fair share of the economic pie.

The absence of political justice, I argue, is a result of the failure of these modern states to establish themselves as legal states in the twin senses of being justified by law and governing through it. Their rulers have had conscious reasons to avoid submitting to the conditions of legality; but this is not the only cause of the nonlegal character of most of these states. An equally significant problem has been the failure of lawyers and judges to become a political class capable of shaping the course of events in their countries.

The reasons for this failure are complex, connected to the strength of the military and secret police, and to economic distortions introduced by oil into the Middle Eastern region in particular. They are also connected, though, to the scholarly class who were the guardians of the law in the classical Islamic state. The lawyers have not, for the most part, sought to emulate or replace these scholars. Under the classical system, the scholars sometimes served the state; but they served the state in the name of the law. By contrast, the lawyers of the modern Muslim world have, with some exceptions, mostly embraced an instrumental, European-origin view of the law and so served the law only in the name of the state.

The failures of the modern states that are to be found in majority-Muslim countries help explain the surprising renaissance of Islam not only as a faith but as a powerful political force in the last quarter century—the topic of Part III. It has been widely noticed that a central theme in contemporary Islamic political argument is the demand for justice, a demand driven both by the language of the Qur'an and by the striking absence of justice in actually existing political arrangements. What has not been as well understood, however, is the intimate link between the demand for justice and the core Islamic political goal of establishing shari'a. In the minds of Westerners and even some secularized Muslims, shari'a often stands for the covering of women and the administering of corporal punishment for thieves and adulterers. But the true meaning of shari'a is, of course, law itself—and just not any law, but the divine Law that governed the Islamic state through the centuries of its success.

The call for an Islamic state is therefore first and foremost a call for law—for a legal state that would be justified by law and govern through it. The advocates of the new Islamic state often say that it was the abandonment of the Islamic legal order that led to the collapse of the traditional Islamic state. Although this is only partly true, it is certainly the case that the abandonment of law as an organizing political force is what doomed the modern, non-Islamic states to fail along the dimension of political justice. The reason why such a broad public in the Muslim world finds the call to an Islamic state so resonant—even when they may not personally wish to embrace a life of rigorous Islamic piety—is that they understand that the failures of their states can be remedied only by a renewed commitment to the idea that law creates the ruler, not the other way around.

The problem with the prescription of returning to the shariʿa is that law itself is not a brooding omnipresence that can be invoked with a word. Law is, rather, a set of social practices, a particular way of using language and reason to deploy force. It can operate only through the regular, repetitive conduct of people acting in concert. The vehicles for such coordinated group action are the mysterious things we call institutions.[9] They include formal government bodies like courts, but they also extend to schools, colleges, and universities where ideas are inculcated and exchanged, and to professional offices where habits and practices are learned. Institutions are no substitute for legal ideas or values, but without them, law is homeless and thus is not really law at all.

So when advocates call for the creation of an Islamic state, they need to figure out what actual institutions will develop and apply the Islamic law they seek to renew. Outside of Saudi Arabia—where the scholars occupy a version of their traditional role in a system rendered radically different from the old one by its oil wealth—the class of the scholars as it once existed in the Sunni Muslim world has been decimated.[10] It would today be impossible simply to announce that the scholars were being returned to their traditional role as keepers of the law. In

Shi'i Iran, Ayatollah Ruhollah Khomeini dealt with this problem by introducing a vast range of new, scholar-dominated institutions when he gave life to the revolutionary Islamic state. Khomeini did revive the position of the scholars.[11] But instead of restoring the balance between the ruler and the scholars, he sought to merge these two separate institutions under a single supreme jurist-ruler—and the failures of the Islamic Republic of Iran are the legacy of this megalomaniacal mistake.

That is why today's Islamists—those who seek to design the new Islamic state—do not call for the resumption of the authority of the scholars. In the Sunni world, they typically see the scholars as they exist now as weak and compromised, simultaneously co-opted by unjust regimes and rendered toothless by them. In Shi'i-majority Iraq, the fear is that the Shi'i scholars may overreach in the Iranian manner. What is more, although contemporary Islamists are committed to the idea of divine law, many also want to draw upon democratic principles, and the idea of conferring substantial political power on unelected scholars usually does not seem very appealing to them.

The approach taken so far by governments that are trying to create themselves as new Islamic states has been to adopt the structures of liberal constitutional democracy and to try to fuse them with Islamic principles. The written constitutions of both Iraq and Afghanistan, for example, guarantee equality for men and women and boast elected legislatures with lawmaking power. Both set up high courts with the power to declare that laws violate the constitution. Both, though, establish Islam or Islamic law as the principal source of legislation.[12]

This arrangement is very different from putting all legal power into shari'a courts. Neither the Iraqi nor the Afghan constitution does that. Instead, they follow the well-established trend in the Muslim world of giving the shari'a courts jurisdiction only over personal matters such as marriage, divorce, and inheritance. In other words, the new Islamic states are not seeking to re-create the institutional authority that the scholars held in the old Islamic state. They are, rather, adopting an experimental approach of *democratizing* the shari'a by calling on the legislature to draw upon it in passing laws. Once adopted, those laws would have validity and force primarily because the legislature enacted them, not because they came from God. This is an attempt—however underdeveloped—to make the legislature into an institution that would engage with the ideal of law, not just the application of power.

Similarly, the constitutions of Iraq and Afghanistan both prohibit the legislature from passing any law that violates core tenets of Islam. In effect, this amounts to the *constitutionalization* of the shari'a. The highest judicial bodies in these countries will have the power to say definitively whether ordinary laws passed by the legislature do or do not contradict Islam, just as they rule on whether ordinary laws violate the principles of the constitution itself. These courts are certainly being conceived as institutions with responsibility to Islamic law. Their responsibility, however, arises obliquely: their job is not to begin by saying what Islamic law requires, but rather to evaluate legislation that has been challenged and only then issue an opinion as to whether that legislation conforms to the dictates of the shari'a. And they have this responsibility because the constitution says so, not because it inheres in the shari'a itself.

The democratization and constitutionalization of the shari'a contemplated by the new Islamic states represent an attempt to resuscitate the Islamic state as a legal state through institutions that would both justify it by law and allow it to govern through law. But they introduce in a powerful new way a tension that was much less salient in the constitutional thought of the classical Islamic state: the potential conflict between divine law and human law. The scholars who shaped the classical constitution were very well aware that human law existed. They acknowledged the right of the ruler to enact binding regulations that did not contradict the shariʿa, and they also were closely acquainted with tribal, customary laws that in some places provided most of the legal regulation necessary for organizing daily life. But the formal structure of their constitutional theory was that the shariʿa authorized these other types of law, and that these laws could under no circumstances contradict the shariʿa as they interpreted it. In this way, the scholars allowed for the existence of plural types of law without conceding their power as sole interpreters of the fundamental law that authorized the others.

In the new Islamic state, what is going on is more complicated. From the perspective of the shariʿa as a totalizing legal methodology, it can be claimed that the written constitution of the state is legitimate only to the extent that it makes the shariʿa paramount. This viewpoint would assimilate the new Islamic state into the logical structure of the old. But from the standpoint of the written constitution, matters are much less clear, because the meaning of the shariʿa is explicitly being made the province of the legislature and the courts of the state.[13] This confusion—does the shariʿa come before the state or the state before the shariʿa?—is in fact a version of a familiar problem in the constitutions of liberal states. Americans have never fully resolved the question of whether the inalienable rights of life, liberty, and property preexist the U.S. Constitution or derive from it. It is more than possible to run the constitutional system of a legal state without resolving this thorny and ever-controversial difficulty.

The greatest challenge facing the new Islamic constitution derives from the uncertainty about identifying who is in charge of specifying the meaning of the shari'a and by what authority. In the old Islamic state, it was the scholars, and their authority derived from the shariʿa itself. But who is it to be now? Is it the public, who elects the legislature? If so, what authorizes the public as a whole to interpret the divine law? Is it the legislature itself, authorized by the constitution? What about the judges of the high court? Finally, let us not forget about the scholars themselves, who still exist today, albeit in much reduced circumstances.

In a book published just before U.S. troops entered Iraq in 2003, I argued that it was in principle possible to resolve the tensions between Islam and democracy by means of a constitution that was both Islamic and democratic.[14] Whatever the disastrous practicalities of governance in Iraq or the limitations of the central government in Afghanistan, the constitutional processes in these two countries demonstrate that a constitution of Islamic democracy is indeed possible. The question I am raising here is the logical sequel to that claim: can the new Islamic state succeed?

The answer, I conclude, depends on finding an institutional authority with the capacity to stand up and check executive power in the name of the law. If the new Islamic state can find an institution to fill the role traditionally played by the scholars, it has a reasonable chance of establishing political justice and, through it, popular legitimacy. This could be a legislature, if it can succeed in climbing out from under the weight of executive dominance to oversee and limit executive power. It could also, in theory, be a judicial body exercising the power of constitutional review and supervisory authority over a legal system freed of systemic corruption.

Each of these options will be extremely difficult to accomplish for Islamist political parties seeking to gain a share of power. If they win elections outright, Islamists are subject to the same temptations and distortions that face any other victorious political movement. If, as is generally the case, they gain power piecemeal, they will face opposition not only from still-powerful executives in their own countries, but from Western nations suspicious of the Islamist program in its domestic and foreign-policy manifestations.

If Islamists take the reins of government but cannot manage to institutionalize the balance of powers and restore the rule of law, we are all in for a rough ride. The aspiration to an Islamic state will be there, but, like the Islamic Republic of Iran, the state will end up disappointing its supporters and alienating the rest of the world. Isolated and angry, it may turn against its own citizens or outward against its neighbors, both near and far. Just now, the Islamist promise of the rule of law offers the only prospect for meaningful political justice for many Muslims. If it, too, fails, the alternative may well be worse.

I

WHAT WENT RIGHT?

The Call for a New Islamic State

NOT ONLY Western experts but the educated classes of the Muslim world have been astonished over the last quarter century at the rise of a political movement calling for the creation of Islamic states in majority-Muslim countries. That many governments in Muslim countries are badly in need of reform is not in doubt. Especially in the Middle East, dictatorships and monarchies have failed to bring economic prosperity, military dominance, or even basically legitimate government. But why has this sorry state of affairs not led to the emergence of domestic political movements seeking the creation of liberal democracy as we saw, for example, in Eastern Europe? What is different about the Muslim world?

Deepening the mystery of the rise of a distinctively Islamic political vision is the fact that, for most of the twentieth century, the standard view among most experts both in and outside the Muslim world was that the classical Islamic state had failed. Islam, on this view, was the organizing principle of the Ottoman Empire, as it had been the basis for the Islamic dynasties before it. The Ottoman Empire had collapsed under the weight of its own backward-looking worldview, plunging the peoples who had lived under it into a shameful period of colonial subjugation. By the end of the twentieth century, it was obvious that the nationally organized states that succeeded the Ottoman Empire had not performed very well themselves, and that their distinctive brand of nationalism and state socialism was on its way out. But why should that have directed a frustrated public back in the direction of the form of government whose failure had opened the door for this sorry chapter in Muslim history?

Most observers who have set out to answer this question have emphasized the perception in the Muslim world that secularism was bound up in the failure of nationalist state socialism.[1] Meanwhile, over the course of the twentieth century there had always been a few voices consistently calling for a return to Islam as the solution to political problems. For the most part, they had not been heeded, but once everything else had failed, more people began to ask: why not give Islam a try?

There is much to this account of the rise of Islamic political views to the forefront in recent years. If one notices that, for thirteen hundred years, Islam provided the dominant language of politics in the Middle East, and if one treats the twentieth century as a brief aberration, the argument gains still more force. Then the reemergence of Islam looks like a return to the norm, and the rise of a secular nationalism looks like the historical phenomenon in need of special explanation. The extraordinary capacity of Islam to generate a language of justice also helps explain its great value to people seeking to resist governments that are plainly unjust. But even this richer account fails to fully explain the goal that is always placed first in the political platform of those who call for an Islamic state: the restoration of the shari'a to its central role in Islamic society.[2]

Indeed, to hear the Islamists tell it, the shari'a is precisely what makes the state Islamic. Consider the simplest and most eloquent slogan of the Islamist movement: "Islam is the solution." Taken out of context, it sounds fanciful and naive.[3] How could Islam alone reverse deep problems of political dysfunction and economic stagnation? To the Islamists, though, and indeed to their intended audience, "Islam" means the shari'a, understood as an all-encompassing structure that precisely orders social relations and facilitates economic justice. As if to bring the point home, some Islamists also insist that "Islam is our constitution." Again, the claim makes little sense if taken as an abstraction. But to understand the shari'a as a constitutional ground rule is to invoke a rich and complex history of constitutional law and theory that stretches back centuries.

In essence, then, the call for an Islamic state is the call for the establishment of Islamic law. Once we take this demand seriously, we can begin to understand why so many people in the Muslim world find themselves attracted to Islamic politics. Looking at their own states, they see clearly that power, not law, is structuring political, economic, and social relations. They simultaneously see that their states are broken. Law sounds as though it might be a solution. What is more, law seems to hold particularly great promise because, in the collective memory of the Muslim world, it is still dimly remembered that the classical Islamic state was a state that was governed by law and that governed through law.

The Birth of Islamic Law

To Westerners, and even to those Muslims educated under Western-influenced conditions, it may sound extremely strange to describe the classical Islamic state of the Ottoman Empire and the many dynasties that preceded it as fundamentally legal. Western writers have for centuries gone to great lengths to describe the Muslim world as the home of Oriental despots who did what they would, free from the constraints supposedly imposed on Western rulers. In fact, many of the most enlightened, law-loving Western thinkers—Montesquieu is one famous example—used the image of the Islamic East as a literary device for projecting their vision of the worst possible nonlegal regime.[4]

For the most part, they did this not out of hatred or spite, but simply because every good political allegory needs a contrast between a utopia and a dystopia. Even sophisticated thinkers like the great German sociologist Max Weber used Islam in something like this way. When Weber wanted to describe judgment handed out without legal rules of decision, he used the image of the Muslim qadi sitting under the palm tree, dispensing justice as he saw fit.[5]

Nothing could have been further from the truth.[6] The qadi was supposed to judge according to law, and when he did not know the law, he was supposed to refer the inquiry to a qualified jurist who would answer in the form of a fatwa, a legal responsum.[7] The roles of both the judge and jurist were carefully defined by law and by custom. The judge would have been appointed to his post by an official charged with this task and responsible ultimately to the caliph, who sat at the top of the legal structure of the Sunni Islamic state. The jurist, for his part, would have earned the title of mufti, conferring the right to issue fatwas, after a rigorous education at the hands of more senior scholars who reserved the right to authorize their students to engage in this formal legal practice.[8]

The self-regulating community of scholars expert in the law was as much a part of the legal system as was the judge, who was usually appointed from among their ranks. But unlike judges, who became part of the state apparatus by accepting a caliphal appointment and what pay came with it, members of the scholarly class were not named by anyone connected to the government. They became scholars by education and deportment, and their status was determined by the reputation they enjoyed among their fellow scholars.[9] And it was as scholars,

not as judges, that they exercised their exclusive right to explicate God's law.

How did this arrangement come about? How did the scholars, men with little direct political power, no armies, and often
no government posts, become the sole keepers of the shari'a,
and hence the only meaningful check on the power of the ruler?
The answer goes back to the way Islamic law itself developed
alongside the Islamic state.

In his lifetime, the Prophet Muhammad was both the religious and the political leader of the community of Muslim believers. His revelation, the Qur'an, contained some laws, per-
taining especially to ritual matters and inheritance; but it was
not primarily a legal book and did not include a lengthy legal
code of the kind that can be found in parts of the Hebrew Bible.
When the first generation of Muslim believers needed guidance
on a subject that was not addressed in the revelations they had
heard, they went directly to Muhammad. He either answered
of his own accord or, if he was unsure, awaited divine guidance
in the form of a new revelation.

With Muhammad's death, revelation to the Muslim community stopped. The joint political-religious leadership position
passed to a series of caliphs who stood in the Prophet's stead.
The Arabic word *khalifa* ("caliph" is an anglicized version)
means a substitute or stand-in.

It appears that some of the earliest caliphs may have thought
of themselves as stand-ins for God.[10] That would presumably
have given them enormous authority to speak on God's behalf,
even if they did not claim to receive prophecy. Within a few
generations at the outside, though, it became accepted that the
caliph was a stand-in for God's messenger, Muhammad, and
not for God. That left the caliph in a tricky position when it
came to resolving difficult legal matters. The caliph possessed
Muhammad's authority, but not his direct access to divine reve-

lation. It also left the community in something of a bind. If the Qur'an did not speak clearly to a particular question, how was law to be derived?

The answer that developed over the first couple of centuries of Islamic rule was that the direct revelation of the Qur'an could be supplemented by reference to things that the Prophet had done or said in his lifetime—collectively, his path or *sunna*. These actions and words were captured in an oral tradition of reports passed from one person to another, beginning presumably with someone who witnessed the action or statement firsthand. But of course even a report (*hadith*) deriving from a particular factual situation cannot answer most legal problems that arise in future cases. For that it was necessary to reason by analogy from one situation to another. There was also the possibility that there might be a communal consensus about what to do under particular circumstances, and that, too, was thought to have substantial weight.

The fourfold combination of Qur'an, the path of the Prophet as captured in the collections of reports, analogical reasoning, and consensus amounted to the basis for a legal system.[11] But who would be able to say how these four factors fit together? Indeed, who had the authority to say that it was these factors and not others that formed the sources of the law? The first four caliphs, who knew the Prophet personally and were leading a rapidly expanding empire that was focused more on conquest than on governance, might have been able to make this claim for themselves. But after them, the caliphs were faced with a growing group of persons who asserted that they, collectively, could ascertain the law from the available sources. There comes a point in the birth of every legal system at which someone must make a foundational assertion that he is entitled to say what the law is. And there is safety in numbers. The self-appointed group who asserted authority to identify the law came to be known as the scholars—and over the course of a few generations, aided no doubt by the need for an organized legal system in a large empire, they got the caliphs to acknowledge them as the guardians of the law.

The Heirs of the Prophet

The exact process whereby the scholars simultaneously created Islamic law as a distinct category and established themselves as its definitive interpreters remains somewhat obscure.[12] That is not at all unusual for the origins of a legal system. The history of legal systems is often murky, and so it is always desirable for the class that controls the law to act as though it has always been in charge. In English common law, the judges dealt with this problem of origins by claiming that the law itself ran back to a time out of mind of man.[13] For the Islamic scholars, the opposite assertion applied. Men's memory did run back to the time of the Prophet, and indeed memory was the crucial source of the sayings that provided evidence about the Prophet's path. The simplest thing to do was to act as though, from the moment of the Prophet's death, there had always been proto-scholars gathering accounts of his practice and reasoning from these to legal conclusions. In some sense this must surely have been the case, since people always need to resolve concrete disagreements. It seemed natural for the scholars to understand stories of property disputes between, for example, the Prophet's daughter Fatima and Abu Bakr, the first caliph, in terms of legal principles that were assumed to have been at work in them.[14]

Not that the scholars naively assumed that everything said about the Prophet was true. Relatively early in Islamic history they began trying to distinguish between reliable reports and those that may have arisen by error or fabrication. As reports proliferated, memorized in the thousands by increasingly specialized transmitters, it became increasingly important to sort out good from bad.[15]

Eventually there developed a set of criteria for doing so, based largely upon the chain of transmission of the reports from one transmitter to the next, which were conveniently incorporated and memorized alongside the reports themselves. By the time collections of the reports were being written down (now more than three centuries after the events recorded in them), there was said to be a "science of reports" evaluating the characters of the transmitters, their reliability, and the soundness of the entire chain, which could not be stronger than its weakest link. Evaluating reports regarding the Prophet was just one component of legal study. But from the scholars' perspective what mattered was that, like other pieces of the legal reasoning process, it remained their exclusive preserve.

In charge of both assembling the relevant legal materials and interpreting them, the scholars could truly be called, in the words of one report, "the heirs of the prophets."[16] Technically speaking, the scholars could not make the law. Only God could do that, and only prophets could report that he had done so. According to a theological doctrine broadly embraced among Muslims, Muhammad was "the seal of the prophets," after whom no revelation would be forthcoming. That left the scholars to interpret and apply God's law. In theory, the scholars discovered the law in a manner not entirely unlike that of English judges who claimed to discover the common law by reasoning from ancient precedents. In practice, though, both sets of judges were as good as making the law—not by total invention, but through the tremendous power of interpretation.

Over time, different schools of legal thought among the scholars coalesced around certain key figures whose influence stretched over particular geographical areas that were under Islamic rule.[17] Markers of a mature legal system, the schools of legal thought had an institutional component that emerged from their intellectual cohesion. A young scholar could attach himself to a particular school, which meant learning the doctrines of that school and committing himself to following those doctrines when it came to issuing actual legal rulings. The different schools were aware of each other, and they often defined their doctrines through a kind of indirect dialogue. The greatest scholars typically preserved the right to decide an issue based on the teachings of one of the schools to which he did not belong, or by looking outside of the school doctrines altogether and back to the original sources. But for most ordinary jurists, the obligation to stay within the doctrinal constraints of his own school created a certain amount of regularity and predictability. After all, one thing that makes a legal system effective and lawlike is that the decisions of legal actors are shaped or even determined by the legal materials they have in front of them and the authoritative techniques of interpretation recognized by the system itself.

Scholars and Caliphs

Legal institutions like the schools do not develop in a political vacuum. For law to be practically relevant, as opposed to purely abstract or theoretical, it must have some connection to the way power is deployed by those in authority. Although Islamic law was "jurists' law" in that its content was determined by the jurist-scholars,[18] and not the state, it was also state law in that it had a mechanism for being enforced by the state. That mechanism was the judiciary, appointed by the caliph and serving under his direct authority.

Under the theory that the scholars developed to explain the division of labor in the Islamic state, the caliph had paramount responsibility to fulfill the Qur'anic injunction to "command the right and forbid the wrong."[19] This was not a task he could accomplish on his own. It required him to delegate responsibility to, among others, judges who would apply God's law as interpreted by the scholars. To be qualified as a judge, one was required to have an understanding of that law, even if one did not need to be able to solve every complex legal question on one's own. It followed that judges should be drawn from among the scholars. When acting as judges, they would be implicitly fulfilling the caliph's will to follow the law. They served at the caliph's pleasure, and he could promote or fire them as he wished. That did not mean, however, that they would follow the caliph's legal interpretation, except perhaps insofar as they were drawn from the legal school to which the caliph adhered. Judicial authority came from the caliph, but the law to be applied came from the scholars.

This subtle arrangement is of the utmost importance for understanding the balance of power between the scholars and the caliph. Some students of the classical Islamic constitution have argued that the scholars could offer no meaningful check on the ruler because the caliph retained the power to appoint and fire judges, and through this could exercise influence on the law as he wished.[20] But this view tends to elide the power to choose judges (and thereby affect the outcomes of cases) with the power to make the law.

Law—particularly jurists' law—consists of much more than what the judges decide in particular cases. It contains also the considered opinions of scholars outside the judiciary about the content of the law and its application. The scholars expressed their views in legal treatises, and also by issuing fatwas in response to questions put to them by individuals or by judges who were having difficulty determining what law to apply in a given case. The corpus of law as shaped by the scholars was known to the members of the scholarly community, including judges. The law, in this sense, was a real and almost tangible force, embodied in the collective experiences and opinions of the scholarly class.

As a result, if the ruler were to pressure judges to violate the law in deciding cases, it would become clear to the scholars that he had done so. The ruler might be able to use pressure and his appointment power to get the results he wanted in particular cases. After all, judges were still individually much weaker than the ruler, even if they belonged to a class that was stronger than themselves. But the ruler could pervert the course of justice only at the expense of being seen to violate God's law.

The cost of breaking God's law was not trivial. According to the theory of government promulgated by the scholars, the very purpose of the ruler—his reason for being—was the enforcement of divine law. To break the law, then, was to demonstrate that one was unqualified to rule. A ruler might get away with the occasional lapse. A sustained pattern of lawbreaking over time, however, would show those in the know that the ruler was not fulfilling his function on earth.

But did it matter? What capacity did the scholars have to rein in a ruler who no longer deserved to rule? This question is all-important if we want to make sense of the balance of power in the classical Islamic state. The academic answer often given is that the scholars were essentially powerless vis-à-vis the ruler, and that they accepted this powerless position as a matter of practical reality.[21] As one important historian has recently put it, although the shari'a functioned as a constitution, "the constitution was not enforceable," because neither scholars nor subjects could "compel their ruler to observe the law in the exercise of government."[22]

But this answer, I want to suggest, does not sufficiently account for the subtlety of power relations in a constitutional state. It is rarely the case that *any* constitution enables judges or nongovernmental actors to "compel" the obedience of an executive who controls the means of force. The means whereby the executive is constrained by institutions without the power of the sword are always more subtle, and by necessity and design are driven by words and ideas, not forcible compulsion. In fact, the scholars had several important tools at their disposal for keeping the ruler in line. To see what they were, we need to examine both the way the scholars themselves talked about their authority, and the ways they acted in the real world, which were not always identical to what they said in their books.

To hear the scholars tell it, the law itself gave them the right to appoint the caliph and to dismiss him. The standard books of constitutional law—written, of course, by scholars—asserted that the caliphate was not hereditary as of right. A caliph could be either designated by his predecessor, or else appointed by a group of electors described as responsible for "binding and loosing" the community as a whole. This group was supposed to ascertain that a candidate deserved to hold the office. Then its members were supposed to form a contractual agreement with the candidate through which they promised their allegiance to him. In return, he was obligated to follow the law. Some scholars argued that a caliph designated by his predecessor still needed the approval of the electors. According to all the scholars, though, the electors were the scholars themselves.

The constitutional law books also specify that a ruler who fails to uphold justice or becomes disabled in a way that interferes with his duties is disqualified from continuing in office. Concerned about maintaining political stability, the scholars were in general cautious about asserting openly that they had the right to declare that the ruler was disqualified. One scholar reported that "many people"—he did not say who—"believed that a wrongdoing and oppressive caliph should be deposed."[23] But the implication was present in the idea of binding and loosing. The scholars had the authority to bind the community to obedience. Who else, then, would have had the power to loose it from the bonds of obligation?

In practice, the scholars did not spontaneously declare a sitting caliph disqualified. This would have been a foolish thing to do, especially in view of the fact that the scholars had no armies at their disposal. Nevertheless, the scholars had a substantial capacity to keep the ruler within the bounds of the law. This power derived from the political realities of succession in the medieval Islamic world, realities that both shaped and were shaped by the scholars' constitutional rejection of automatic hereditary succession.

In a system of royal heredity, like that common in medieval Europe, the whole point is to minimize uncertainty about who will take over in a moment of succession. Such a system reduces the need for an institutional body that will decide who becomes king when the previous king dies. A succession crisis should in theory emerge only where there is no obvious heir, or where the heir is impugned as a bastard. By contrast, in a system of designation or election, there are often at any given time multiple claimants to the position of ruler. This creates the need for some person or group of people to buttress the claims of the person who will successfully emerge as the ruler in a transitional situation.

In the medieval Islamic environment, this was precisely the way things worked. Powerful sons or other relatives of the present ruler might be contemplating a palace coup to remove their predecessor. Each potential claimant might also be interested in dispensing with the others. Outside the palace, there could

31

Ibn Taymiya

be other challengers waiting in the wings, poised to take over the state and establish a new dynasty or even to invade the state by force.

This uncertainty about succession made the scholars extremely important. The first thing a new ruler needed was affirmation of the legitimacy of his assumption of rule. This would help consolidate his authority against early challenges from other frustrated claimants. Then, once his position was consolidated, the sitting ruler needed to be able to fend off new challengers and invaders. To do so, he needed to be able to rely on the scholars to assert the continuing legitimacy of his rule. In the extreme case where he faced invasion, the ruler would need the scholars to declare the religious obligation to protect the state in a defensive jihad. Having the scholars on his side in these times of challenge and crisis was a tremendous force multiplier for the ruler who could be said to follow the law.

One famous example of scholarly support of a regime challenged from outside comes from the life of the scholar Taqi al-Din Ibn Taymiya (1263–1328), a prolific and iconoclastic figure who managed to get himself tried, convicted, and imprisoned for his theological and legal beliefs on at least three separate occasions (and who eventually died in prison). Despite his willingness to fall afoul of official doctrine, however, Ibn Taymiya offered staunch support of the defense of Damascus and its Mamluk regime against attack by the Mongols who threatened the city in the late thirteenth century. So closely identified was he with the defense of the state that he is reported to have been present as a kind of military chaplain at the (temporary) defeat of the Mongols outside Damascus in 1299.

What was significant about Ibn Taymiya's defense of the state was the role he accorded to the shari'a in the course of his propagandizing against the Mongol threat. The Mongols professed Islam and so might have had a colorable claim to rule if they conquered. Yet in his capacity as a senior scholar, Ibn Taymiya issued a fatwa in which he declared the Mongols to be infidels, notwithstanding their nominal adherence to Islam.[24]

The central element in Ibn Taymiya's analysis was their failure to adhere to the shariʿa. In particular, the Mongols' use of their traditional, customary law in place of Islamic law came in for disapprobation, because of its direct threat to the supremacy of the shariʿa. Ibn Taymiya held the view that a ruler who failed to act in accordance with the scholars' legal dictates was not supported by the Qurʾan's injunction to "obey those in authority among you."[25] Indeed, for Ibn Taymiya, the fact of nonadherence to the shariʿa vitiated the Mongols' claim to Islamic character and so deprived them of any claim to legitimacy. It followed that resistance to the Mongols was a form of jihad, obligatory defensive war against non-Muslims. The practical consequence of the declaration of jihad was to obligate Muslims everywhere to support the cause of resistance, and to prohibit any accommodation. Ibn Taymiya himself held that political wars among Muslims were prohibited and did not deserve the support of any Muslim; jihad, on the other hand, was a universally recognized duty.

Not every scholar agreed with Ibn Taymiya's position regarding the Mongols. For reasons I shall discuss shortly, many scholars seem to have been prepared to accommodate their rule once Damascus did, in fact, fall into Mongol hands. Ibn Taymiya himself was willing to acknowledge that a basically orthodox ruler could be tolerated even if he made theological or other errors; so long as the shariʿa was followed, scholars should reprimand him and bring him to correct views. But with true infidels—taken to include those who failed to apply the shariʿa—there could be no compromise.

33

If a ruler's adherence to the shari'a could be deployed by the scholars to mandate support for that ruler's legitimacy, then, conversely, a ruler who flouted the law—and by extension affronted the scholars who were its keepers—ran the risk of being abandoned in his hour of need. The scholars could harm the ruler by keeping quiet, or by affirming his legitimacy in tepid terms. In a more extreme case, the scholars could affirm the legitimacy of an alternative claimant.[26] A deposition of a ruler accomplished by force might be accompanied by a fatwa declaring the illegitimacy of the deposed ruler.[27] Naturally, issuing such a fatwa was a risky move until the claimant had won the day. It usually sufficed for the scholars to say little until the new ruler took power, and then validate that ruler as one who possessed the legitimate authority to rule in virtue of his commitment to follow the law. Then the cycle would begin afresh. Without a single soldier under their command, the scholars nonetheless represented a crucial source of power in the Islamic constitutional structure.

In short, the scholars' power to confer legitimacy was significant because the uncertain nature of succession demanded an affirmation of legitimacy. Small wonder, then, that the scholars' constitutional law never authorized succession by the mere fact of heredity, even though some rulers no doubt wanted just that. Of course, insisting on their own ability to elect the caliph would have given the scholars still more power. Allowing succession by designation of the previous ruler was a partial concession to the rulers' power and desire to shape a dynasty. But this compromise still gave the scholars most of what they needed. Designation left room for some uncertainty. The designated heir could be changed at any moment. (In the modern era, King Hussein of Jordan changed his designated successor from his brother to his eldest son just days before he died.) The fact of designation could be challenged much more

34

easily than, say, birth order, the usual method in hereditary monarchies. The presence of at least some uncertainty in the succession process ensured that the ruler and his successors, whoever they might be, would always need the support and validation of the scholars.

In exchange for their conferral of legitimacy, the scholars asked just one thing of the ruler: a commitment to the rule of law. It is important to note that, according to the interpretation of Islamic constitutional structure that I am proposing here, the scholars were neither entirely selfless nor embarrassingly selfish in making this demand. They were reaffirming their own sociopolitical role even as they were serving the greater good of strengthening adherence to the law.

On the one hand, the ruler's promise to respect the law entailed a promise to respect the scholars and their position in society. In extracting the guarantee, the scholars were serving their own collective interest in self-perpetuation as centrally important players in Islamic society. The ruler was handing over to the scholars the design and—through the judges who were drawn from among the scholars—the running of the legal system of the state.

On the other hand, there is every reason to believe that the scholars' self-identification with the law was total and sincere. The scholars did not demand riches, nor did they, like the barons at Runnymede, set out to weaken the ruler as they insisted on their own prerogatives. The scholars' commitment to the law derived from their understanding of it as God's law, greater certainly than the ruler, but also greater than themselves. The ruler's promise to back up the legal decisions of the scholars with force recognized the formal elevation of law over the arbitrary whims of any one individual. This constitutional arrangement made the law supreme. It established, we might even say, the rule of law.

Preserving the Law: Crisis and Solution

The structure of mutual validation in which the ruler affirms his duty to the law and the law in turn recognizes the legitimacy of the ruler is a delicate thing under any circumstances. There is always the risk that the ruler will decide he is strong enough not to need the legitimation conferred by his obedience to legal duty, so that the considerable benefits of flouting the law outweigh its costs. In the medieval Islamic world, the first major crisis that arose to challenge this structure came when the men who occupied the caliphate—that unified symbol of executive authority and divine sanction—began to lose their grip on actual power.

By the middle of the eleventh century, the once-great Abbasid caliphate in Baghdad was in deep trouble. Buwayhid invaders from near the Caspian Sea had conquered much of the large territory of the Abbasid Empire in the later tenth century and continued to dominate those who held the title of caliph. Seljuk Turks were threatening Baghdad, which eventually fell to them in 1055. The caliphal throne of Harun al-Rashid and other storied rulers was in danger. The abolition of the caliphate might well have carried with it the abolition of the law itself, so closely were the two connected.

In this milieu lived the scholar Abu al-Hasan al-Mawardi (972–1058), a preeminent legal figure in his era, who also served as a diplomatic go-between for several caliphs in their negotiations with Buwayhids and Seljuks alike. The core constitutional problem facing Mawardi was to shore up the disintegrating credibility of the caliphate. According to tradition and law, the caliph was supposed to exercise actual executive authority, as had the Prophet and his caliphal successors. But under the Buwayhids—and as it would turn out, under the

Seljuks—this was increasingly unrealistic. These rulers mig̱
be prepared to show the caliphate some respect, but they we..
not prepared to allow the caliph to govern independently.

Mawardi's legal solution to this problem was encapsulated
in a book called *The Ordinances of Government*, probably the
first and still the most important classical Islamic work devoted
solely to constitutional law.[28] Its timing was no coincidence: the
caliphal system was undergoing a transformation. So long as
the norms of the constitutional balance remained unchanged,
no book was really necessary to state what they were. But disorder breeds uncertainty, and it gave Mawardi a reason to try to
make sense of what the rules were and ought to be.

In his book, Mawardi addressed the situation where the caliph is controlled by another person who exercises executive
authority. So long as the de facto ruler follows the principles
of religion and law, Mawardi argued, the caliph may allow the
situation to stand.[29] He also analyzed the case of a provincial
governor who takes power through force, rather than being
designated initially by the caliph. Mawardi asserted that under
these circumstances, it was lawful for the caliph to designate
the self-proclaimed governor as his deputy after the fact, and to
assign him the task of engaging in actual worldly governance.[30]

Of course the reality was the other way around: like the ruler
who dominated the caliph, the self-designated governor was
deciding to acknowledge the theoretical authority of the caliph.
But this fig leaf allowed the authority of the caliphate to continue as a kind of legal fiction. The caliph, said Mawardi, was
still in charge of ensuring that the shari'a was followed. And
the de facto ruler must acknowledge the caliph's authority by
virtue of accepting the position as the caliph's designated man
in charge.[31] In so doing he would undertake to govern according to the shari'a. So in a sense, went the argument, the
caliph was still exercising worldly authority, as the tradition

required—only he was executing it through a deputy. The reason Mawardi gave for allowing the de facto ruler to exercise authorized power was necessity. In the absence of caliphal authority, the public interest would be harmed.

Mawardi laid out his model only in reference to the governor of a province and did not expressly offer the model of deputization to account for the case of the caliph whose executive authority had been usurped even where he lived.[32] But subsequent scholars, most importantly the towering legal, philosophical, and theological writer Abu Hamid al-Ghazali (1058–1111), took Mawardi's view to its logical conclusion. Ghazali, living in Baghdad under Seljuk rule, expressly allowed this very sort of deputization by the caliph of the de facto ruler.[33]

Modern commentators have subjected Mawardi to harsh criticism for relying on a principle of necessity and then inventing the legal fiction that reduced the caliph from a temporal ruler to a kind of Muslim pope—someone who lacked actual governing power but gave his blessing to those who did. In the late 1930s, as Germany's legal and political institutions caved in to the Nazi takeover, the great British Islamicist Hamilton Gibb wrote that "in his zeal to find some arguments by which at least the show of legality could be maintained, al-Mawardi did not realize that he had undermined the foundations of all law."[34]

Seen in the light of the balance of power between the ruler and the scholars, however, Mawardi's constitutional compromise looks ambitious rather than defeatist. Preserving the power of the caliph was not the scholars' objective—brute military facts had already prevailed on that score. Instead, Mawardi was looking for a way to maintain the principle that the shari'a was binding on the ruler. Through the fiction of the caliph deputizing the actual ruler, the submission of that ruler to the law would be achieved. This arrangement offered the new kind of de facto ruler some of the same legitimacy that had been enjoyed by the caliphs—on the condition that the ruler would follow the shari'a.

The result of the de facto ruler's acknowledgment of the shari'a was that it reasserted the role of the scholars as the counterweight to the ruler. Their authority to declare the law and their symbolic embodiment of the shari'a were preserved intact, even as the practical power of the caliph was jettisoned. In effect, Mawardi's scheme sold out the caliph to protect the scholars. The key to making this move palatable was that the scholars were committed, as always, to the cause of the shari'a. The shari'a would survive the decline of the caliphate, which had been designed to serve it; and the scholars would emerge in as good a position as they had previously occupied.

Ghazali's explanation for allowing deputization lends support to this interpretation. For him, the caliphate was the legally necessary condition for the validity of all legal acts—the font of authority from which the practice of the shari'a grew. If the caliphate were to disappear, Ghazali argued, the law itself would cease to operate. Contracts, judgments, testimony before the courts—all would lack the force of law. Such a situation obviously could not be tolerated. The necessity of preserving the caliphate, in form if not in substance, was simply the necessity of preserving the legal system in the face of the decline of the caliphate. Far from undermining the foundations of the law, the legal fiction that the caliph authorized the de facto ruler was in fact designed precisely to preserve the foundations of the law—in the person of the scholars, though not of the caliph.

Mawardi's compromise as extended by Ghazali may be read, then, not as a scholarly concession to power, but as a brilliant maneuver that successfully preserved the law and the scholars in their constitutional position even after the caliphate had failed in its assigned task of preserving orderly government.

If Buwayhids or Seljuks had assumed power without acknowledging the primacy of the shari'a, then all might have been lost. From Mawardi's standpoint, the shari'a was everything; the prerogatives of caliphate (almost) nothing. This was, then, a victory for the shari'a and the scholars who guarded it. To lament the decline of the caliphate or to excoriate Mawardi for permitting usurpation would be to miss the point, which was the preservation of the shari'a. Arguably, it was Mawardi's intellectual foundation that preserved the balance of powers in the classical Islamic constitution for another seven hundred years.

Law and Order

How and why did the scholars' control over the content of the law facilitate the effective functioning of the classical Islamic state? The answer to this question has three components that are distinct and yet related; and each deserves its own discussion. First, a confident, self-defined elite that controls and administers the law according to well-understood and well-settled rules tends to produce predictability and stability across time with respect to the affairs that matter most to most people—the distribution of property. Stability and predictability encouraged investment in long-term ventures and projects. Second, by controlling the law, the scholars could limit the ability of the executive to expropriate the property of private citizens. This in turn caused the executive to have to rely on lawful taxation to raise revenues, which itself forced the rulers to be responsive to their subjects' concerns.[35] Third and finally, the scholars' control over the law had the effect of casting an aura of legitimacy over the system of government that obtained—which simultaneously strengthened the force of any

40

government enactment that could be seen as consist‹
the overall system.

The clearest medieval indication of these interrelat‹
tures may be found in the writing of the brilliant social theorist
Ibn Khaldun (1332–1406). In rough parallel to some Western
accounts of the function of public law, Ibn Khaldun argued
that failure to protect private property from encroachment by
the government removed the incentive to produce. "When the
incentive to acquire and obtain property is gone, people no
longer make efforts to acquire any."[36] Unjust governance, he
explained, was the surest way to trigger the cycle of reduced
productivity that would ultimately destroy a civilization.

Injustice, Ibn Khaldun went on, certainly included "confis-
cation of money or other property from the owners, without
compensation and without cause." But it went further than
that, to include taking property with insufficient compensation, forced labor, unjustified legal claims, the imposition of
duties not required by the shari'a, and unjustified taxes. When
the Prophet forbade injustice, he had in mind preventing "the
resulting destruction and ruin of civilization." That is why the
shari'a "generally and wisely aims at . . . five things as necessary:
the preservation of (1) the religion, (2) the soul (life), (3) the
intellect, (4) progeny, and (5) property."[37] Ibn Khaldun lifted
these five categories from the law books, where they conven-
tionally stated the "ends of the shari'a." In his formulation, a
core purpose of the shari'a becomes the preservation of civilization through the protection of private property from governmental depredation. Law is the bedrock principle on which civilization rests; and the most important worldly function of law
is its aspiration to restrain the ruler from the inevitable temptation to expropriate and exploit.

Despite his powerful account of the crucial social function
of law, however, Ibn Khaldun does not seem to have recognized

the scholars' institutional role in administering the law as the mechanism whereby they entered into the balance of powers. In fact, he was skeptical of the scholars' claim that, as heirs of the Prophet, they played an important constitutional role.[38] The reason seems to have been that Ibn Khaldun's own master-concept of historical change—the notion of group solidarity from which all political authority grows—left little room for power that could not be easily translated into force. Since, as Ibn Khaldun correctly noted, the scholars wielded no such power and were not in practice part of the executive, they did not appear to him part of the essential constitutional structure.

Recognizing that the law as described by Ibn Khaldun functioned only by virtue of its relation to the scholars who administered it yields a more robust view of the scholars' role than the one Ibn Khaldun himself took. I want to argue here that the system of scholarly control over law encouraged stability, executive restraint, and legitimacy. To do so, I must begin by explaining what the legal system did and did not do under the classical Islamic constitution.

In the traditional Islamic state, not every dispute was decided by judges drawn from the scholarly class with reference solely to the principles of *fiqh*, or Islamic legal doctrine. To the contrary, from the very simplest Islamic states to the enormously complex Ottoman Empire, the Islamic constitutional order always included administrative regulations with the force of law that were issued by the ruler or his deputies.[39] Such regulations covered a broad range of subjects: weights and measures, often supervised by a special official (not necessarily a scholar) known as the master of the market; taxation, including taxes not specifically mentioned by the classical Islamic legal sources, which could be administered by tax officials who were not themselves members of the scholarly class; and criminal affairs, in which such regulations sought to resolve difficulties associated with the high standards of proof required by the shari'a before its permitted corporal punishments could be applied. Administrative regulations in the criminal sphere could be administered by nonscholars at the discretion of the ruler and could mandate punishments up to and including the death penalty.

In each situation where administrative regulations were issued and enforced, one could say that the rules that applied to ordinary people in their daily lives were not the rules of the shari'a itself. This has led some scholars of Islamic law to think that the shari'a was not a legal system in the Western sense of the term, insofar as its teachings—especially the learned disquisitions of the scholars—were not always the rules guiding the behavior of government officials in ordinary cases. In fact, in the twentieth century, Western scholars of Islamic law have spent an inordinate amount of time debating the theoretical question of whether Islamic law is really "law" at all.[40]

This question, however, is misplaced—and not only because the participants in the Islamic legal order through the ages would have considered it so. Every society of any complexity at all has norms with the force of law that derive from multiple sources. The question of whether they are part of a unified system of law depends on whether those norms are understood to be subordinate to a single source of authority. The administrative regulations that covered so much of life in the classical Islamic legal world were understood by one and all to derive from the authority of the ruler that was recognized by the shari'a. A regulation could never contradict or supersede the shari'a. By definition, regulations were issued and could be applied to fill the gaps and cover those areas where the shari'a did not lay down any mandatory rule. Thus, as a matter of principle, the complex of administrative regulations was subordinate to the authority of the shari'a—and hence to the authority of the scholars who were uniquely in control of its content. By analogy, one might consider the enormous administrative apparatus of the government of the United States. The executive branch of the federal government issues thousands of commands with the force of law and conducts trial-type proceedings by the tens of thousands; yet it is not understood to have displaced the lawmaking authority of the legislature or the decision-making authority of the courts, because all it does is in principle subordinate to the commands of those bodies and the Constitution.

With this crucial background, one can turn to the effects of the scholars' control of the content of law. The creation of stability and predictability resulted from the broad societal recognition that the law—as embodied in the scholarly class—transcended the particular person of any powerful individual in the society, including the ruler. Such recognition is valuable in any society, because it makes individuals believe that they can buy and sell land and goods, enter into partnerships, or create other important legal relationships without constantly worrying that someone who has more power than they do will step in and steal their profits when convenient.

But stability and predictability are especially valuable in those societies where transition from one ruler to the next can be disorderly and even violent. If one thinks that the next ruler might not respect the distribution of property as it exists now, one will be loath to risk any wealth on deals or agreements that run over time. One will also worry about the all-important question of transferring property to offspring by bequest. The scholars soothed these concerns, because even if the ruler were to change, there would still be scholars—and they would still be demanding that the law be followed. Thus we can observe that even in periods where invasions and changes of power were common—like eleventh- and twelfth-century Andalusia, for example—the same scholarly families continued to serve as judges and administer the law across the generations.[41] Keeping the scholars in control of law was therefore also useful to new rulers, because it enabled them to signal to property-holders that they would indeed respect the property distribution as it existed prior to their arrival in power.

That is not to say that the scholars were unwilling to allow certain changes in the law that corresponded to the positions of new rulers. No legal system, however autonomous, can ever be completely free of influence from other forces in society. It was possible, for example, that the school of Islamic law administered in a given jurisdiction could change to a different school when a new ruler demanded it. This was especially true as increased organization and bureaucratization came to accompany the expansion of the imperial legal order. The Ottomans, for example, brought their favored school of law, the Hanafi school, with them wherever they conquered and consolidated control, and its application marked their ascendance. But even they often preserved the local school alongside the Hanafi, sometimes—as in North Africa—appointing both Hanafi and non-Hanafi judges to administer justice. And in any case, the place of the shari'a was always preserved, thereby assuring the stability and predictability that scholarly control over law promised.

Stable and predictable legal rules, however, would be of limited utility if the ruler were willing or able to circumvent them freely to steal the wealth of his subjects or to punish people who had not broken the law. As Ibn Khaldun put it, injustice of the civilization-destroying type can be committed "only by persons who have power and authority."[42] How did the scholars' control over law operate in practice to constrain the executive, either from expropriating what rightfully belonged to others, or from using his power to create a reign of terror? The question is especially sensitive in light of the ruler's ability to issue administrative regulations to fill the many gaps left by the shari'a itself.

To begin with, it is important to acknowledge that no constitutional structure is immune from structural abuses—and the classical Islamic state must certainly be included in this generalization. There were sometimes corrupt or tyrannical rulers who robbed, stole, and oppressed, despite the best efforts of the scholars. The relevant inquiry is whether these depredations took place inside or outside law, and how effectively the classical Islamic constitutional system operated to reduce the likelihood that these rulers could succeed.

The key to the scholars' resistance against unjust rulers was their ability to insist that the ruler must remain within the bounds of the shari'a or risk being stripped of his legitimacy. The threat of delegitimation—discussed earlier—gave a ruler a significant incentive to try and demonstrate that his actions were within the sphere of his rightful powers. It therefore made sense for him to use his power to issue administrative regulations to enhance his wealth or to punish those who opposed him; and a crucial feature of those regulations was that they could not squarely contradict the shari'a.

With respect to property, this principle operated as a meaningful constraint. In the case of inheritance—probably the most important piece of legal business in every society before the modern era—the shari'a left relatively little room for alteration. The Qur'an itself prescribed rules for heirs' shares, which the ruler could not easily alter to grab a larger share for himself. To deepen the protection of the law, the scholars developed a version of the legal doctrine of the trust. This allowed the transmission of wealth across generations through the creation of charitable foundations that were legally immortal, immune from governmental interference, and included descendants among their beneficiaries.[43] Out of a combination of shrewdness, the foundations often benefited schola¹., tions like schools alongside the heirs whom the founders sought to perpetuate. As a result, to interfere with such a foundation was sure to anger the scholars, who often relied on the foundations for their institutional livelihoods. A ruler who wanted to swallow up a chunk of the property of his best-off subjects would have to contend with the existence of these foundation-trusts, which he disturbed at his peril.

When it came to more ordinary temptations to steal property, the ruler was blocked by the shari'a's acknowledgment of the sanctity of private property and its corresponding prohibition of theft. A ruler who could not simply steal to enrich his treasury had to tax to do it. Here the shari'a offered him slightly greater latitude. On the one hand, it recognized certain canonical taxes: the alms tax for the poor; the "Fifth" tax mentioned by the Qur'an as God's due and interpreted by the scholars as lawfully collectible on booty, mining, and some other forms of income; and the poll tax administered to non-Muslims resident in the Islamic state.[44] On the other hand, the shari'a did not squarely prohibit the raising of other supplementary taxes on an administrative basis, so long as the canonical taxes were collected.

Within this rubric, a ruler could still choose to impose harsh and even confiscatory taxes. The difficulty he would face was exactly that faced by any overtaxing ruler: the public will pay only for so long before becoming restive. The manuals of guidance for kings written by worldly political advisers in the Muslim world—and carefully read by Ibn Khaldun, who as we have seen also condemned overtaxation—naturally warned kings against the unpopularity and potentially disastrous economic effects of overtaxation. But the scholars' writings restrict themselves to explicating the canonical taxes and say little in the way of prohibiting special taxes that might otherwise be created by the ruler. The real effect of the shari'a in the context of revenue generation is to shape the ruler's preferences so that taxes become his best option; the result was to encourage rational rulers to exercise their taxing power cautiously.

The system of criminal justice worked somewhat similarly. Just as Islamic rulers needed extracanonical revenue to support their government's activities, no ruler could expect to administer justice successfully by relying solely on the criminal punishments laid down in the shari'a. The problem was not primarily their limited scope—murder, theft, and sexual immorality, after all, covered most of the categories of the criminal law in the premodern world. The problem, rather, was the standard of proof demanded by the shari'a before punishment could lawfully be meted out.

Harsh, corporal punishments are a familiar—probably the most familiar—feature of the shari'a. According to the classical Islamic law, the thief will lose a hand by amputation, and adulterers will suffer death by stoning. What is not generally known to Western audiences, however, is that these punishments may not be administered except after conviction by a court under a standard of proof so high that it can only very rarely be met. In the case of adultery, for example, the sexual act itself must be witnessed by four adult males of good character who testify to the facts. Such circumstances are, one may safely assume, extraordinarily rare.[45]

The reason for a legal system to combine extremely harsh punishments with a high standard of proof is that law enforcement is expensive. Before the modern era, no society had what we would today call a fully developed police department, and the classical Islamic constitutional order typically had just a handful of officers responsible for enforcement of ordinary laws. Extreme and visible punishments serve as salient reminders to the public to follow the law. More important, if the odds of being caught and punished for wrongdoing are low, as they typically will be in a society without a police force, then the punishment must be set high to produce something approximating the right amount of deterrence. The corporal punishments of the shari'a were clearly designed originally for such a world of very limited enforcement—much like the English common law that punished every felony with death.

Over time, however, as Islamic states (particularly the Ottoman Empire) became more extensive and developed increasing control over ordinary life, reliance on a handful of harsh punishments came to seem an inadequate basis for social control. As in the modern world, it seemed that security and effective administration would be better served through criminalization of a broader range of conduct, enforced by lesser penalties requiring a lower standard of proof. Administrative regulations were again the tool used to accomplish this goal. They could not replace the criminal punishments of the shari'a, but they could supplement the shari'a punihments so extensively that they came to constitute the bulk of what an observer would call the actual criminal law of the Islamic state. No scholars were necessary to explicate these regulations, and the standards of the shari'a court, with its requirements of multiple witnesses of good character, could be relaxed or even ignored. Rulers typically did rely on courts to apply this administrative criminal law, so the scholarly class did preserve some role in the functioning of the de facto legal system. Nevertheless it was not technically necessary for a ruler to use courts to apply his regulations.

Given that the ruler could go outside the shari'a to punish wrongdoing, in what sense did the scholars' control over law constrain the ruler in the criminal realm? Part of the answer is that the regularity of the shari'a courts and procedures provided a yardstick by which the framing and applications of administrative criminal regulations could be judged. By continuing to write and theorize about the punishments of the classical shari'a-based criminal law, the scholars suggested that a properly functioning judicial system followed rules and principles regarding the proof of criminal conduct. This is probably the reason why so many rulers did rely upon scholars and courts to administer their own legal system.

Legitimacy and Bureaucracy

There is a further and perhaps deeper answer to what was assured by the scholars' control over law. Because the shari'a as interpreted by the scholars ultimately authorized the ruler to issue administrative regulations, the scholars preserved the theoretical idea that these regulations were indirectly authorized by the shari'a—and hence by the scholars themselves. The scholars had little choice but to acknowledge that a complex urbanized society could not easily be administered through the application of only the handful of criminal-law rules and principles of the classical Islamic law. The regulations were therefore necessary, and the ruler would have to issue them. Far better for the scholars to treat them as subject to the general approval of the shari'a than to challenge them or characterize them as solely the product of the ruler's whim.

The upshot of this strategic decision was for the scholars to legitimize the regime of administrative regulations created by the ruler to enable the functioning of ordinary social control. Again, a useful analogy may be drawn to the rise of the administrative state in the United States in the twentieth century. The new administrative entities displaced in many ways the traditional, exclusive role of the courts in the federal system. But because it would have been unrealistic to reject all these new institutions as illegitimate challenges to their authority, the judges instead blessed them while claiming to retain the power to review their decisions, albeit deferentially.[46] The scholars in the classical Islamic constitutional order continued to act as though they were authorizing the social order that was in fact increasingly governed by the ruler.

In so doing, the scholars reaffirmed the formal element of their own position, while simultaneously offering legitimacy to the new institutions being developed by the increasingly complex Islamic state. As the state grew and developed, there were inevitable reductions in the importance of the scholars. Nevertheless the scholars did retain enough prestige and significance through their legitimation function so that they were able to constitute some kind of counterbalance to the otherwise unfettered ruler. The clearest example of this complex process may be seen in the gradual bureaucratization and centralization of the scholars' function in the Ottoman Empire.[47]

In pre-Ottoman Sunni constitutional tradition, as I have noted earlier, the ruler appointed judges from among the scholarly community, but the power to control the content of the law remained with scholars who often did not hold any official government function. These nongovernmental scholars shaped the content of law through legal treatises and teaching, but most centrally through the fatwa, issued in direct reply to a legal query by a judge or a party engaged in an actual case. As the Ottoman legal system developed, the imperial court went beyond the traditional practice of appointing judges and began in addition to create the novel position of the official mufti, or fatwa-issuer. The post may have begun as honorific merely, but in time it took on legal significance, and the fatwas issued by the official muftis came to have a binding character. (Traditionally, in the pre-Ottoman model, no one was bound by a fatwa and it remained for the judge to decide among competing fatwas should they exist on a question.)

The grand mufti also took on the job of authorizing others to act as lower muftis. Eventually a substantial legal bureaucracy was built up around the *shaykh al-islam*, as the grand mufti was called. The most famous and important occupant of the office, the sixteenth-century scholar Ebu's-su'ud Effendi (Abu al-Sa'ud), who has been studied extensively, issued thousands of fatwas in the service of Suleiman the Magnificent.[48] Some of these were recognizably fatwas in the traditional sense of legal opinions on uncertain questions, but others were closer to judgments about the outcome in particular cases. Ebu's-su'ud and later grand muftis came to employ numbers of law clerks who reviewed cases and made recommendations that could be accepted with a penstroke that turned them into official pronouncements—a practice much more like that of a chancery or even a modern appellate court than that of the pure type of the classical mufti with his considered, individualized legal reasoning.

The bureaucratization of the post of grand mufti was paralleled in the development of the rest of the Ottoman legal system. In place of the informal system of scholarly education and authorization, there arose a formal career path with designated steps that a scholar must follow to hold government office.[49] The legal functions of the scholarly community came to be carried out by scholars who were entrenched within government-sanctioned institutions. The law, then, increasingly came within the scope of the state; it gradually lost some of the autonomy it had preserved under the classical system in which scholars were effectively independent unless they assumed judicial office.

This slow process of incorporation into the state's apparatus was a risky strategy for the scholars. As we shall see in Part II, it paved the way for the epochal moment of Ottoman reform in which the Sunni scholars were stripped of much of their jurisdiction and lost their capacity to counterbalance the ruler. But that disastrous occurrence (disastrous at least from the standpoint of the scholars) took place nearly three hundred years after the peak of Ebu's-su'ud's career. It is crucial to notice that the scholars had much to gain from their relation with the Ottoman imperial state—and that for an extremely long period, their strategy was by their own lights successful.

An expanding global empire with a growing central administration needs an effective and unified legal system to keep its house in order and ensure economic growth. The Ottomans, that is, needed law, as had the Romans before them. By the same token, the Ottoman sultan had at his disposal mighty armies raised by draft, and a palace guard drawn from an elite class of royal slaves whose loyalty ran directly to the sultan. He had a literate secretarial class that kept his imperial accounts and were developing techniques of administration across distance. Had the sultan wanted to administer solely through regulation and abandon the scholars, he could perhaps have imagined it possible to do so, as later reforms would ultimately reveal. By allowing themselves to be brought into the expanding state apparatus, the scholars kept themselves—and the shari'a for which they stood—relevant to the imperial enterprise. They brought the shari'a with them to newly conquered lands, in the Balkans and beyond. They kept the Ottoman sultans in the Islamic fold. In short, for centuries, they kept official Sunni Islam alive.

What was in it for the sultans was the power of legitimation that the scholars could and did provide. The Ottomans, non-Arab Anatolians who treated Arabia as a minor province, embraced this Islamic legitimacy enthusiastically. Beginning with Suleiman, the Ottoman sultans had themselves declared caliphs, notwithstanding the express constitutional requirement of Arab, Qurashi descent, which they lacked.[50] As caliphs they assumed (theoretically, at least) the mantle of responsibility for preserving the shari'a. The scholars were proof of their fitness to the task. The scholars thus enabled the Ottoman sultans to claim for themselves the leadership of the entire Sunni world, a claim accepted at face value by Western observers right up until the end of the caliphate and, more remarkably, taken seriously for much of Ottoman history by most of the world's Sunnis.

As the price of this legitimation, the scholars insisted upon some measure of executive limitation. Islamic law was in principle the law of the empire—and that meant the sultan was subject to the law, not above it. The sultans' unprecedented power enabled them to introduce unprecedented bureaucratic institutionalization of the scholarly class, but the sultans nevertheless accepted the yoke of the law as interpreted by the scholars—a position of subservience to law otherwise unheard-of in the annals of great empires. Justinian's great *Digest* stated that "[t]he prince is not bound by law."[51] No less powerful or extensive in their reach, the sultans earned the caliphate at the price of accepting that God and his law were above them.

Government by and under law was therefore a meaningful and important aspect of life in the Ottoman Empire until its final years. The point is not to deny corruption or rule by decree, both of which can coexist under some circumstances with the rule of law, even in a modern Western state. Rather, relevant government officials decided disputes through law. Government collected revenue pursuant to established taxes, rather than through ad hoc expropriation. Criminal law was administered by courts following regulations that could not contradict the rules and principles of the shari'a. And the ruler acknowledged the law as supreme over him.

Under these bonds of law, the Ottoman Empire flourished for as long as any of the great world empires have done. When its decline came, and reform was desperately needed, that reform took aim at the law. The consequences of this reform attempt—not only for the empire, but for the entire Sunni world—form the subject of Part II.

II

DECLINE AND FALL

Ottoman Reforms

THE DEATH of the classical Islamic constitution is intimately intertwined with the decline of the Ottoman Empire—and the efforts to reverse that decline through reform and modernization. Despite military reforms undertaken in the 1820s, the empire in the last years of Sultan Mahmud II saw the most serious military setbacks that the empire had suffered in generations—the loss of Greece, cemented by the defeat of the Ottoman navy by British, French, and Russian ships at the Battle of Navarino in 1827, and the loss of Algeria to French invasion in 1830. By the time Mahmud's son, Abdulmecid I, took power in 1839, elites within the empire had become convinced that internal reform was necessary. Indeed, in that year Abdulmecid faced the very direct embarrassment of having to rely upon five major Western powers to avoid ceding substantial portions of his territory to Mehmed Ali, nominally the governor of Egypt but actually a competing ruler in his own right.

The impulse to reform derived from the sense that outward weakness reflected inward disorder. Ottoman officials, some educated in the West, attributed Western successes in part to effective and improved internal administration. These were, after all, the years in which Western bureaucracy, with its sharply defined responsibilities, high quality record keeping, and use of statistics, was becoming an extraordinarily powerful tool of government. Meanwhile the Ottoman bureaucracy, once the best in the world, had not undergone any fundamental reform since the sixteenth century.

The Ottoman reformers also felt pressure from the West.[1] The empire needed credit, and borrowing from the West meant reassuring Western governments and markets of the empire's fiscal responsibility. Both as creditors and as sometime-allies concerned with preserving the international balance of powers, Western states wanted to see the sick man of Europe healthy enough to function—though not, of course, so hardy as to function as a major threat to any of them.

Between 1839 and 1876, these varying impulses produced a series of reforms known collectively as the Tanzimat.[2] These included military reforms and changes in the mechanisms of taxation, which were crucial to the goals of getting the empire back into strong financial and military condition.[3] Most important, the Tanzimat period saw important juridical reforms, the effects of which turned out to be far greater than anticipated at the time they were put into place. For our purposes, these reforms may be divided into legal and constitutional innovations. The former category includes codification, meaning the reduction to rules of the content of the shariʿa. The latter category comprises institution making, meaning the creation of previously unknown institutional bodies and their introduction into the preexisting constitutional order.

Together, I shall argue, these legal and constitutional reforms displaced and destroyed the scholarly class, without leaving in their wake any institution or social entity capable of counterbalancing the executive as the scholarly class had once done. The consequences of the displacement of the scholars were world-changing. It opened the possibility of secular government; but simultaneously, the removal of the one meaningful check on executive authority cleared the way for autocratic and absolute power—which soon became, in much of the Muslim

kanun

world, the dominant mode of government for most of the twentieth century. The resulting governance disasters, I shall argue in Part III, themselves eventually fueled the desire to return to Islamic government once again.

Legal Reform and the Problem of Codification

In the classical Sunni constitutional balance, the shariʿa existed alongside a body of administrative regulations that governed many matters in the realms of taxation and criminal law. The Ottoman Empire had long featured thousands of such regulations, called *kanun*, a word whose derivation from the Latin *canon* testified to its origins outside the shariʿa.[4] The earliest Ottoman legal reforms took those administrative regulations, which existed in scores or hundreds of separate pronouncements, and codified them into a limited series of unified documents.[5] The scholars raised little fuss about these codes. They appeared to fall within the authority of the ruler to promulgate administrative regulations, to which the scholars had long since reconciled themselves. Thus these early codes did not, on the surface, challenge the authority of the scholars any more than previous such regulations had done.

Some of these early Ottoman legal codes followed European models in substance. The Penal Code of 1858, for example, followed the French criminal code. But more important, all followed European models in their form. They proposed to give the user—presumably, a judge or legal officer—a comprehensive set of rules to govern cases that would come before him. The impulse to codification in Europe was based in large part upon the desire to regularize the administration of justice by sparing the relevant legal decision-maker from having to know an enormous and complex body of law. Codification brought these rules together for easy consultation by an official who would more closely resemble a modern bureaucrat applying rules found in a single source than a traditional judge interpreting disparate legal authorities. This phenomenon was probably not threatening to the scholars in the Ottoman Empire because they had already accepted the notion that the administrative regulations could be applied by persons other than judges. The early Ottoman codes, by focusing on matters formally outside the scope of the shari'a, seemed to pose no direct threat to the scholarly class.

The same cannot be said of the next and far more dramatic step of Ottoman codification: the comprehensive code of the civil law of the shari'a known as the Mecelle (Arabic *majalla*) and produced by a distinguished committee of scholars and experts between 1869 and 1876. The Mecelle represented something new in the history of the shari'a. By tradition and logic, the shari'a was an uncodified body of legal doctrines, principles, values, and opinions. It was the province of the scholarly class to use interpretation and discern the requirements of the law. The fact that the law could not be looked up and ascertained by just anybody was precisely what made the scholars into the keepers of the law and its embodiment. Their store of knowledge, their judgment, and their techniques of interpretation actually constituted the law itself. The code purported to replace of all these with a list of rules.

It is often said that a judge applying the rules laid out in a legal code has substantially less discretion than does a judge whose job it is to interpret an amorphous set of legal materials such as we find in a common law jurisdiction. In fact, there is reason to think that even the application of codified rules requires interpretation that can confer substantial discretion even if the participants in the legal system pretend none exists. Regardless, the social meaning of the task performed by a legal officer applying a code differed profoundly from that of a judge interpreting a broad body of law. A legal officer applying the rules found in the code is simply a necessary vessel, a tool for the lawmaking authority to apply its general rules to particular cases. The more automatic his process of application, the better (and fairer) the system is. As a cog in the legal machine, his identity and importance are minimized: anyone qualified should be able to perform the job. In a modern bureaucracy, the parts should be interchangeable, or as close to it as possible.

A judge interpreting a broad set of legal doctrines and principles, however, plays by definition a central and significant role in the legal process. As the mediating force between the abstraction of Law and the particularity of the case, he literally comes to embody the law itself. He is the master of specialized knowledge that is intimately connected to the construction of the law. Even if he is devoted to the notion that the law is divine and that he merely discovers it, the discovery belongs to him— or rather to the community of interpretation that authorizes the discovery.

It follows that the transformation of the shari'a—from a body of doctrines and principles to be discovered by the human efforts of the scholars to a set of rules that could be looked up in a code—effected a corresponding transformation in the social meaning of the role of the scholars as keepers of the law. In the classical era, a person asking the question "Where is the law?" in the Islamic world could be answered only by an interlocutor's pointing to the scholars and saying, "The shari'a is with them." After the Mecelle, the same question could be answered by pointing to the code itself—not to those empowered to apply it. Codification therefore sounded the death knell for the role of the scholars as keepers of the law. The aspiration to codification obviated the traditional need for the scholars. It took from them their all-important claim to have the final say over the content of the law.

The source of the problem was not solely that the interpretive role was so different from the role of applying codified rules. The other reason that codification deprived the scholarly class of its role was that when the lawmaking body usurped the scholars' final authority over the law, it shifted the locus of ultimate legal authority. What had remained for centuries in the hands of a quasi-independent class of scholars now passed into the ambit of the state.

Under the classical Islamic constitution, the condition for the administrative regulations was that the shari'a authorized the ruler to issue these regulations. Ultimate authority rested with the shari'a. The regulations had legal force, theoretically speaking, because the shari'a allowed them to exist. But by issuing the Mecelle, which purported to state the content of the shari'a, the executive implied that the shari'a itself had authority only insofar as it was incorporated into a legal document issued by the ruler and his state. This was a historic reversal, even if its effects were not immediately apparent. Ultimate authority now rested not with the law, but with the ruler.

Had this implicit feature of codification been apparent to the scholars at the moment the Mecelle was issued, one would expect there to have been greater objection to it than seems to have occurred. The objection could have taken one of two forms. The scholars could have argued that the act of codification was itself impermissible because only they had the authority to declare the content of the law. Or they could have argued, more theologically, that when the state codified the law, it was usurping God's role as the source of all law. To issue legislation on matters within the purview of the shari'a could have been considered blasphemous, as it has sometimes been described by subsequent Islamists. Either objection, had it been raised by the scholars, might have led them to notice that their own position in the legal-constitutional order was being placed in serious jeopardy.

But the scholars who were active in the Ottoman Empire at the time of the issuance of the Mecelle seem not to have raised these objections, at least not very forcefully. The sitting grand mufti did briefly succeed in having the drafting of the code transferred to his office and out of the Ministry of Justice. But his concern seems to have been about controlling the process of codification, not blocking it, since one volume of the sixteen-volume Mecelle (a volume later rescinded when control went back to the ministry) was produced on his watch.[6] The codification process lost momentum after the constitutional reforms petered out; but by then the damage had been done.

Why was the scholarly opposition to codification not more absolute? With a century of hindsight, the relative acquiescence of the Ottoman scholars seems deeply mystifying. Epochal change was taking place right under their noses; and the scholars had precisely the right incentives for vigilance—the usually potent combination of institutional self-interest and religious belief.

Experts on the period have addressed this question without quite answering it definitively.[7] In any event, explaining nonaction is one of the hardest challenges the historian can face. People generally leave some traces describing why they have done something significant, but it is quite rare for them to leave direct evidence stating why they have neglected to do something that in retrospect seems to have been enormously important. Nevertheless, it is possible to offer some partial explanations for the scholars' silence in the face of the dramatic changes wrought by the Mecelle.

For one thing, members of the scholarly class, selected by the grand mufti, were included in the body that drafted the code, and its rules reflected Islamic legal doctrine. Some of the commission members, including the chairman, had background and training both in classical Islamic law and in the modern, Western-influenced law that was already being taught at the university in Istanbul.[8] The inclusion of scholars was intended as a signal to the scholarly community that the new project would incorporate their wisdom, not replace it. After all, the code was not some imitative project undertaken under colonial conditions. The content of the Mecelle as drafted reflected the legal rules of the shari'a, not imported Western legal norms that might conceivably have excited the scholars' ire. The Ottoman Empire was in need of reform, but it was a sovereign entity and a world power, and this part of its legal code followed its own Islamic traditions, in substance if not in form.

As if to underscore the scholars' central role, the code adopted legal rules derived from the Hanafi school of law favored by the official scholars of the empire. The spread of Hanafi doctrine had traditionally been one of the markers of the success of the scholars within the Ottoman Empire. The adoption in the code of the scholars' favored legal doctrine must have seemed like a vindication of their preeminent place in the world of Islamic law. One of the distinctive features of codification is that it cannot easily accommodate a plurality of different legal views on a given question. Under the traditional model, the schools of Islamic law could and did differ on a range of doctrinal questions. All opinions remained valid, at least for adherents of the particular school that adopted each. A code, though, forces a choice between different doctrines, and the one selected as definitive gains a formalized advantage over the others. Later Ottoman codes would attempt to incorporate the best of various schools, but the Mecelle did not.[9] The expressly Hanafi doctrinal choices of the Mecelle may therefore have offset the losses to the scholars in general with gains for the official Ottoman scholars in particular.

As for the potential objection that a code issued by the state and backed by state power usurped the role of the scholars as interpreters, and perhaps even the place of God as the source of law, this concern may have been minimized by the fact that, as originally enacted, the Mecelle was not presented as the exclusive source of law that had to be applied in all circumstances by the courts.[10] Judges as well as muftis—the official scholars to whom it would fall to apply the code—were in principle able to draw upon other sources of law that had not been captured in the Mecelle but were traditional parts of Islamic legal interpretation. The fact that the code was, in theory, not exhaustive left open the possibility that it was not a pure set of laws issued by the state, but a tool for judges that usefully collated and collected rulings drawn from generations of judgments and validated by their origin as part of the shari'a itself. There was, in Islamic jurisprudence, a familiar genre of books that collected earlier rulings for the use of active judges; one student of the period has suggested that the Mecelle may have looked a bit like one of those books "in new packaging, but now with the state behind it."[11]

The addition of the state was, however, no small difference. Even if we can accept that the Mecelle presented itself as confirming and collecting the rules of the shari'a rather than making law, we still need to explain why the scholars did not find the state's act of issuing the code more troubling than they did. Probably the heart of the answer lies in the way that scholars were already deeply imbedded in the bureaucratic and institutional structure of the Ottoman state. Before the Ottoman period, the scholars were to an important degree independent of the state's bureaucratic apparatus. Some scholars might be appointed judges, but what made them *scholars* was ultimately the consensus of their own scholarly class. Equally important, the basic process of declaring the content of the law was largely accomplished by scholars outside government service through their treatises and fatwas.

As we saw in Part I, however, the Ottomans innovated with respect to the institutional separation of scholars and state by creating the phenomenon of the official muftis under the authority of a grand mufti. The official scholarly class still preserved some of its independence over more than three centuries,[12] but the fact remains that a scholarly class integrated into the state was likely to see itself as part of the reform process, not as a potential victim of it. Although the law was, to the Ottoman scholars, formally independent, and although the scholars retained in theory their special position as interpreters of the law, the institutional incorporation of these scholars into the state helps explain why the scholars did not anticipate the devastating consequences of codification for the law or for themselves. Had the scholars considered themselves fully independent of the state—had they retained their predecessors' skepticism about governmental service—they might well have attempted to impede the codification project, instead of aiding it. But the change in their position vis-à-vis the state had happened centuries before, and by the time codification came around, the scholars did not know what was hitting them.

Constitutional Change: The Replacement of the Scholars

Codification in its modern sense does not entirely eliminate the need for judges. Someone must have the job of applying the code, and even if that job is sometimes imagined as essentially bureaucratic, nevertheless most Western legal systems have continued to insist upon legal training for special bureaucrats who hold the title of judge.[13] Codification alone, therefore, need not have devastated utterly the scholarly class, who could have been transformed into a judicial class. Scholar-judges would no longer have had the special role of discovering God's law, but they could at least have retained some of their lost dignity as designated official interpreters charged with applying the provisions of the code.

But the scholars did not manage to retain even this role, at least not in the Sunni Muslim world. The judicial function was eventually taken up instead by a new class of judges trained in modern law, which is to say Westernized law. Unlike the scholarly class, the new judges had no tradition—however attenuated—of independence from the state. To them, Law emanated not from God but from government; and as we shall see, this worldview often translated into a reluctance to treat the organs of the state as subordinate to the law. As a consolation prize, the scholars retained jurisdiction over family law, central to personal life, though not typically to the life of the state.

How did this happen? How did the class whose role was central to the legitimation of the state in the classical Islamic constitutional order come to be reduced to the status of special masters in the family courts? Although the answer certainly begins with codification, it would not be complete without consideration of the equally basic constitutional reforms of the Tanzimat period. Neither would we be able to explain the distinctive constitutional structure of most modern secular states in the Muslim world, with their frequent characteristic of autocracy unopposed by any politically viable force other than the Islamists.

All the major constitutional pronouncements of Ottoman reform took the form of declarations by the sultan of changes he intended to effect or rights he intended to confer as a matter of grace. The two imperial rescripts of 1839 and 1856 are prime examples of this approach. Drafted by senior bureaucrats with a careful eye to their reception in European capitals, each reflected the underlying constitutional assumption that the sultan was acting of his own accord, not subject to the will of anyone other than himself. Insofar as these rescripts did not encroach upon any principles of the shari'a, the classical Islamic constitutional theory would have validated such enactments. In form they did not differ from other administrative regulations issued by the sultan.

These rescripts gave rise, however, to new institutions, whose status was harder to pin down in constitutional terms. The 1839 document was followed by the creation of a "supreme council for judicial regulations," a body that both acted as a court of appeal and drafted new legislation. Its members were unelected, but they made their decisions by majority vote. The sultan agreed in advance to abide by those decisions, thereby creating a body with real (if constrained) decision-making authority. Eventually, after several experiments with different distributions of power, the successor institution was split in 1867 into two bodies, one legislative and one judicial-appellate.

When their authority is juxtaposed with the issuance of the various Ottoman codes, it can be seen that these new institutions went very far toward displacing the scholars' traditional function of declaring the content of the law. The constitution of 1876 went much further.[14] It created two elected legislative bodies, a chamber of deputies and a senate, with responsibility for lawmaking. Courts were authorized separately, to be staffed by judges whose qualifications would be specified by law. A single provision declared, in an almost circular fashion, that affairs touching upon the shari'a would be tried by shari'a tribunals—the only mention of traditional Islamic courts anywhere in the document.[15] The same provision restricted civil affairs to the civil courts.

In this new constitutional arrangement, the notion that the scholars or even their courts were keepers of the shari'a was preserved only in the vestigial sense that the shari'a courts kept jurisdiction over the shari'a. The notion that the shari'a was supreme overall, validating or legitimating the entire constitutional order, was absent. The Ottoman constitution of 1876 was the first self-described constitutional document issued anywhere in the Muslim world.[16] So it would not be an overstatement to say that the arrival of written constitutionalism in the Muslim world marked the beginning of the end for the Islamic state.

The constitution was Islamic in the limited sense that it declared the sultan to be the "Supreme Caliph" and in this capacity the protector of the Muslim religion.[17] It also made Islam the state religion, while guaranteeing free exercise of religion and some further privileges for religious minorities.[18] But the very fact that the constitution made these declarations showed that the authority of Islam was being presented as subordinate to the authority that was issuing the constitution itself.

And the constitution was not promulgated in the name of the people of the empire. Like the imperial rescripts before it, it was the act of the sultan himself, and none other. Sovereignty was vested in his person; and, tellingly, he was pronounced above the law.[19] God's authority over him was neither mentioned nor acknowledged, except by the use of the term "caliph," nor was there any hint of the thousand-year tradition that considered the scholars as God's delegates keeping the law in their charge. This was a modern, Western-inspired constitution in treating the sovereign as supreme;[20] and it was not an Islamic constitution, in that it did not make Islam into a supreme source of authority.

Neither was the Ottoman constitution of 1876 a democratic constitution, because sovereignty rested not with the people but with the sultan. At the same time, the constitution promised a shift in the democratic direction. It did so via the mechanism of the general assembly with its two separate houses. This was, properly speaking, the first legislative body designed along Western lines to be created in the Muslim world. Its members were guaranteed freedom of expression and freedom to vote as they chose. Although a bill passed in both chambers would still require imperial assent to become law, the constitution certainly contemplated an essentially legislative body. The upper house was to be made up of senators nominated by the sultan and serving for life. The lower house, known as the chamber of deputies, was to be elected every four years. Representation was realized on the basis of one deputy for every fifty thousand males.

Taken in the context of the later part of the nineteenth century, the legislature created by the Ottoman constitution looks as though it might have marked a decisive turn in the direction of constitutional monarchy that several European countries were in the process of making as well. An elected legislature, of course, is not at all the same thing as the acceptance of popular sovereignty. Nevertheless, a constitutional document recognizing that the power to make law resided in a body that was at least partly elected was a common feature in what we would now call the process of democratization in Europe. It is certainly possible to imagine that the introduction of such a body into the Islamic constitutional sphere might, over the long term, have had an effect somewhat similar to that produced by its introduction in the West. Eventually, traditional ideas about the source of law—whether divine or royal—might have given way to the notion that the people represent the ultimate source of lawmaking authority.

The result of such a development might have been that the Ottoman Empire in its waning days, and perhaps by extension the Sunni Muslim world more broadly, would have begun an effective transition to constitutional democracy. Such reform certainly would not have sufficed for the alliance between the Austro-Hungarian Empire and the Ottoman Empire to prevail in World War I. And it would be going too far to claim that successful democratic reform would have enabled the Ottoman Empire to survive its defeat. The French and British victors would have been just as intent on dividing the territory of the Ottoman Empire into their own respective spheres of influence had the empire been on the road to democratization. Rather, the consequences of the emergence of a successful and effective legislature in the later years of the Ottoman Empire would have been to introduce into the Islamic context the idea of the elected legislature as a constitutional institution powerful enough to counterbalance the executive there.

Some clarification of this key point is required. On its own, popular sovereignty is insufficient to create a constitutional order in which powers are balanced. The people themselves may become dictatorial if the institutions that represent them—say, popularly elected legislatures—are not counterbalanced by some competing institutional force. This is one powerful constitutional interpretation of the failures of both the English and the French revolutions, in which regicide cleared the field of competition for the legislative body, which then encountered the temptations and distortions of governing without substantial constitutional counterbalance.

But when constitutional democracy did emerge successfully, especially in Europe, legislatures did not come to absolute power overnight. Instead, legislatures gained power through competition with kings who themselves claimed substantial or even absolute powers. The long-run trend in the nineteenth and twentieth centuries—at least where things went well—was for the legislatures to acquire more and more power at the expense of declining monarchies. From a constitutional perspective, struggle between competing sources of power is actually salutary, because some sort of balance remains even as the distribution of power shifts. Legislatures might begin their existence as mild checks upon otherwise all-powerful kings, and they might end up wielding authority rather close to that with which the kings began, checked only mildly by remaining constitutional monarchs. But if neither institution could attain a complete supremacy, the progress from monarchy to democracy had a chance of proceeding relatively smoothly.

In the Islamic constitution, as we have seen, the balance of powers was between the sultan as executive and the scholars as keepers of the law. The innovation of an elected legislature was almost sure to entail the displacement of the scholars, whose unique function of discovering the law through the interpretation of God's word was devastatingly undercut by the introduction of a human source of legislation. Codification, as I have argued, undermined the scholars practically and theoretically. As a lawmaking institution, the legislature would have been as devastating as the codes—perhaps more so.

Yet precisely because the legislature was likely to replace the scholars as an institutional source of lawmaking, it also held out some hope for the balance of powers in the reforming Islamic constitution. In short, the legislature could have *replaced* the scholars as the institutional balance to the executive. Instead of moving directly from the traditional Islamic constitutional balance to full popular sovereignty, the route could logically have passed through the more familiar Western model of balance between the legislature and the executive. In this possible world, the disappearance of the scholars as a significant constitutional force might indeed have been a salutary development, allowing the emergence of a modern, policy-oriented legislative body that would gradually, as in Europe, have insisted upon greater authority vis-à-vis the executive and laid the groundwork for a constitutional democracy.

The plausibility of this vision helps explain why Ottoman reformers were eager to marginalize the scholars. To these reformers, trained in the West or least influenced by Western models, the institution of the legislature looked (correctly, as it turned out) like the engine of successful modernizing reform. The ability to make new laws to meet changed circumstances was an essential part of why the legislature seemed so attractive and promising. To the Ottoman reformers as to modern law reformers everywhere—Jeremy Bentham is the most prominent exemplar of the type[21]—one of the most frustrating difficulties that had to be overcome by law reform was the intransigent and irrelevant traditionalism of the older legal order. The Ottoman reformers no more expected the scholars on their own to transform the law into an effective tool of governance than did Bentham trust the common law judges to make the rapid changes needed to rationalize the laws of England.

To the reformers, then, the shari'a was an impediment to legal modernization, and the scholars, as its keepers, deserved to be removed from their important institutional place in the constitutional order. Their replacement with an elected legislature would, in principle, put modern, younger men (the reformers called themselves "the young Ottomans") in control of the legal agenda, in place of the muftis who stood for tradition. Had the legislature created by the Ottoman constitution of 1876 emerged as a viable and important institution, this modernizing strategy might well have worked. Yet this is where constitutional tragedy struck.

75

The Missing Legislature

As it turned out, the sultan was not unaware of the way that legislative bodies tend to increase their power at the expense of the executive. Sultan Abdulhamid II promulgated the constitution in December 1876 as his first major act after taking power in the wake of a messy transition. (His immediate predecessor took office in a coup d'état but lasted just a summer.) Elections followed almost at once, and the legislature convened in March 1877. It wasted no time in taking the first steps of any legislative body finding its feet: exercising its freedom of speech to criticize the government, and seeking oversight of government ministers.[22] On February 14, 1878, less than a year after the legislature first met, the sultan suspended its operation—and for good measure, he suspended the constitution as well. That was the end of the legislature. Abdulhamid reigned until 1908–9 without ever calling it back into existence, or indeed relying on the constitution in any overt way.

In suspending the legislature and the constitution, however, the sultan did not return to the classical Islamic constitution that existed before the Tanzimat reforms. The Mecelle and the other legal codes remained in place. Abdulhamid did seek to remind the public of the Islamic legitimacy of his office, and the scholars at his court were religiously conservative.[23] But what is certain is that he did not restore the scholars to the constitutional position they had occupied prior to codification. He did not need to do so, any more than he had felt the need to maintain the legislature as a check on his authority. Somehow, Abdulhamid found himself in the position of a near absolute ruler.

The reason this happened is significant. It seems that Abdulhamid was able to consolidate authority as effectively as he did, without having to reinstate the scholars' constitutional position to gain their support, because the scholars had been so effectively displaced in the course of the reform period that they were willing to embrace a ruler who paid them even the slightest attention. It was historically characteristic of the scholarly class that it was willing to accept what it could get in order to try to uphold the principles of the shari'a. But never before in Islamic history had the position of the scholars been so weak. As a consequence, never before did a ruler have to concede so little to the scholars to gain their support.

Over the long run, the consequences of this profound weakening of the scholars turned out to be of extraordinary importance for the constitutional balance of powers. During the period of reform leading up to and culminating in the constitution of 1876, codification was transforming the shari'a, and the legislature was poised to replace the scholars. With the suspension of the legislature and the constitution, the power to declare the law stayed out of the hands of the scholars, where it had traditionally resided—but it did not shift to the legislature, where it might have engendered a balance of powers with the executive. Instead, the power to declare the law ended up *in the hands of the executive himself.* This power, as transformed during the reform period, went far beyond the authority to issue administrative regulations. It had become, in robust form, the legislative power itself—the power not only to supplement, find, or declare law, but to make it.

Paradoxically, through the suspension of the constitution, the sultan actually validated and emphasized his authority as the absolute sovereign that the constitution formally acknowledged: if the sultan could grant the constitution, the sultan could also take it away. At the same time, Abdulhamid managed to reassert his authority without making the corresponding concession of some legislative authority to a legislative body. The reforms, in other words, displaced the scholars as a constitutional counterbalance without successfully replacing them with anything else. The result was an executive freed from the traditional constraints offered by the scholars, yet also untouched by the modern constraints that would have been imposed by a popularly elected legislature.

This neat trick enabled Abdulhamid to rule unfettered for some thirty years. These years were not models of good government. Characterized by autocratic and often arbitrary rule, they included the first stages of what would come to be seen as a genocide against Armenians living at the borders of the crumbling empire. Ultimately, Abdulhamid was deposed in a coup, this time by the Young Turks, whose ideology would eventually give rise to modern Turkish nationalism and the radical secularism of Ataturk.

According to the interpretation of late Ottoman constitutional history that I have just offered, codification and the creation of the legislature combined to take away from the scholars their traditional role as keepers of the law. Once ultimate law-making power came to be located within the state, the scholars lost the theoretical basis for their position as the ultimate source of legitimation for the entire constitutional order. Once legal decision making shifted away from scholar-judges, their practical basis for providing legitimacy to the entire system was eroded as well. The fact that the Ottoman legislature was so short-lived did not restore the scholars to their traditional position. To the contrary, it meant that no constitutional counterweight to executive authority arose to replace the scholars.

In the absence of either the scholars to interpret the law or a popularly elected legislature to enact it, the law came to be conceived simply as the command of the sovereign. Judges trained in the new, state-issued law generally understood their position in much the same way that modern European judges applying their own legal codes did: they saw themselves as

faithful servants of the state. Unlike the contemporary
pean state, though, the late nineteenth-century Ottoma
was not itself a differentiated entity in the sense of incorporat-
ing popular and monarchic institutions. The state was, in effect,
the executive—and nothing more. With the executive as the
source of law, and the judges charged with applying the law
conceived as servants of the executive, the state became a totalizing sovereign entity such as never existed before in Islamic
history.

The Lawmaker State and the Shari'a

In what follows in this part of the book, I shall argue that the
paradigm of the executive as a force unchecked by either the
shari'a of the scholars or the popular authority of an elected
legislature became the dominant paradigm in most of the
Sunni Muslim world in the twentieth century. Beyond this his-
torical-constitutional claim, I shall argue further in Part III that
the distinctive distortions of many Muslim states in this era
were products of unchecked executive authority, and that the
call for the restoration of the shari'a in contemporary Islamist
politics may be seen in substantial part as a response to this
constitutional defect.

In order to advance these claims, however, we must first address a historical complication. Defeat in World War I led to
the fall of the Ottoman Empire. Because the states that were
created to replace it fell under varying degrees of colonial guidance or control, none of them adopted precisely the form of
the constitutional order as it existed in the final decades of the
empire. It is therefore not a simple or obvious move to argue
that late Ottoman constitutional developments—as opposed to

colonialism or other features of modernity—were definitive and formative for most of the Sunni world in the postwar era.

The best way to navigate this difficulty is to clarify the core claim advanced here: that the source of the unchecked executive power in so much of the Sunni Muslim world in the twentieth century was the decline of the scholarly class, coupled with the failure of any comparable balancing institution to replace it. That pattern is most readily visible in countries that were formerly Ottoman possessions, especially Arabic-speaking countries. But it is also true that in the nineteenth and early twentieth centuries, the scholars declined in varying degrees in some areas of the Muslim world that were not under direct Ottoman control; and the problems of those societies, where executive power also tends to be disproportionately unchecked, may be traced to this analogous decline.

In Egypt, for example, quasi-independent under Mehmed Ali, and a de facto British colony after 1882, the process of codification and the decline of the scholars may be observed running roughly parallel to developments in the Ottoman context.[24] Egypt's lawyers, it must be said, made a more serious attempt than those of any other Arab state to become a distinctive political class with a commitment to constraining the executive. Lawyers led the various political parties that demanded independence, and lawyers drafted the 1923 constitution that aimed to create a limited monarchy subject to the rule of law.[25] But the constitution was never effective, and the military coup of 1952 put an end to the lawyers' aspirations. In South Asia, the British Raj also codified Islamic law to some degree;[26] and although Pakistan as it emerged in 1948 was distinctive in many respects, its scholarly class also never enjoyed the sort of constitutional role that its predecessor played under the Mughal Empire some two and a half centuries before.

My argument, then, does not rest upon straightforward constitutional continuity between the Ottoman Empire and its successor states. It depends instead on the continuity between the new role for the shari'a that was introduced in the late Ottoman period and the role played by the shari'a in postwar regimes throughout the Sunni Muslim world. Once I have sketched this continuity, I shall introduce an exceptional case to test the rule: Saudi Arabia, with its distinctive preservation of some version of the traditional Sunni constitution.

The core claim for continuity relies on a set of related observations. First, in the traditional Sunni constitutional order, the shari'a was a transcendent, divine source of law interpreted exclusively by the scholars; but in the late Ottoman period, and in the constitutional orders that prevailed through most of the Sunni world after World War I, the shari'a became instead a set of rules defined and applied by authority of the state. In many cases, the jurisdiction of the shari'a shrank to encompass only matters of family law. Second, the scholars went from quasi-autonomous keepers of the law to, at best, dependent state functionaries. At worst, the scholars turned into purely religious figures irrelevant to adjudication or to governance more generally. Third, as a result of the first two changes, the scholars ceased to be necessary to legitimate the existing government.

These developments in the post–World War I period took place under colonial or quasi-colonial conditions, so it is important to contextualize them in terms of colonial interests and paradigms. Nevertheless, the transformation of the role of the shari'a had already occurred in the later Ottoman Empire. Codification and the displacement of the scholars by the sovereign state embodied in the executive took place under the Ottomans. Although Western influences were important in these changes, the reforms were undertaken under the authority of the sultan.

The Western powers who shaped government in so many parts of the former empire after World War I were building upon a paradigm already put in place by the Ottomans.

Begin with the conception of the shari'a as a set of rules administered by authority of the state rather than as a transcendent source of divine law. Postwar written constitutions in British and French protectorates typically treated the shari'a as just another set of legal rules to be applied by judges appointed by the state. The Iraqi constitution of 1925, for example, established a constitutional monarchy in which the legislative power was vested in an elected parliament.[27] Following the Ottoman constitution of 1876, the monarch promulgated the constitution.

Alongside civil courts, the Iraqi constitution created religious courts that were charged with jurisdiction over family law matters only, which were to be decided according to the school of law favored by the parties before the court. Although the shari'a with respect to family law was not (yet) codified in Iraq—a development that did not occur there until 1958[28]— the authority to apply the shari'a was, by assertion, conferred in the constitution. The shari'a did not serve as the background Law validating the state. Instead it was the other way around: the state, through its official pronouncements, validated application of the shari'a.

In Egypt, the transformation of the shari'a into a set of state-enforced rules was even more complete. Between 1936 and 1942, one of the greatest figures in modern Arab legal thought, 'Abd al-Razzaq al-Sanhuri, took up the task of producing comprehensive legal codes, civil and criminal, which would reflect Islamic as well as Western input.[29] This extraordinary undertaking would have a major impact elsewhere in the Sunni Arab world as other states adopted versions of Sanhuri's codes. The ideological presumption of the project was that the shari'a was

a set of rules associated with Islamic tradition that were susceptible of being loaned to a general legal system where they would
coexist with Western legal rules. Although Sanhuri's project
may plausibly be characterized as in a sense colonial and also
as a kind of resistance to colonialism,[30] it would certainly have
been unimaginable without the precedent of the Mecelle and
the other Ottoman codes, which first reduced the shari'a to a
set of rules.

Seen in the light of the new codes, the collapse of the status
of the scholars was drastic. Now the best judgeship a scholar
could get was administering family law—a position of relatively
low prestige in accordance with its limited jurisdiction. The
civil courts with their wider jurisdiction offered greater power
to their judges. Once the shari'a came to be seen as a set of
codified rules, a judge without training in classical Islamic law
could apply it. This phenomenon was seen, too, in British colonial contexts where direct rule was being used. In India, British
judges had applied codes of Islamic and Hindu law where they
considered it appropriate.[31] In the context of countries where
the judiciary was made up entirely of Muslims, the substitution
of secular-trained civil judges for the scholars made it still
clearer that the Ottoman codification paradigm was being
pushed to its logical limits, and that the scholars no longer
enjoyed a privileged position in regard to applying the shari'a.

As for the scholars' autonomous control over the content of
the law, the idea of the independent scholar issuing fatwas for
the use of the courts had already declined in the Ottoman period. Now even the position of official mufti became increasingly unimportant. Once the shari'a was in effect state-issued,
its interpretation was no longer the unique preserve of the
qualified and trained expert. True, those scholars who sought
to codify the shari'a still had recourse to the writings of scholars. Sanhuri was learned in classical Islamic law, and his codes

drew upon this knowledge. But the scholars whose opinions were sought tended to be long dead.[32] Those few who continued to write on topics of Islamic law increasingly did so in an environment where what prestige they might accrue could not be translated into legal or political capital.

There was, in other words, an enormous difference between writing on abstract and theoretical topics of jurisprudence in a world where the shari'a was nominally the source of all legal authority, and dealing with those same topics in a world where the shari'a was reduced to a set of subordinate legal rules. In the classical Islamic constitutional order, a scholar who wrote a treatise about some topic of jurisprudence that would never be applied in practice was enhancing the intellectual prestige and preeminence of the law. Even true jurists' law served the social function of reminding scholar and layman alike that the shari'a was supreme, and that the scholars were its authoritative interpreters and guardians.[33] Once the state ceased to acknowledge the shari'a as its source of legitimation, writing about theoretical topics in jurisprudence just seemed obscurantist.

This sense of irrelevance drove a perception of the scholars as purely "religious." Contrary to a myth perpetuated by some Western and some Muslim observers, the classical Islamic constitutional tradition was always able to distinguish religious concerns from worldly ones. But the distinctions that the scholars drew never treated religion as wholly disconnected from things of this world, since religion conceived in the Islamic sense assumed for itself the authority and responsibility to demand compliance with all legal duties. The shari'a was therefore classically understood as religious in origin and orientation, yet simultaneously directed toward the governance of ordinary behavior through legal norms. The scholars, by extension, were not merely men of religion but also men of the world, some of whom took on the responsibility of applying the shari'a, and all of whom at least reflected on the relation between the shari'a and practical affairs.

In the environment of state-issued law, however, the scholars' relation to rules whose meaning they did not control looked more like a spiritual interest than a practical one. To wear the garb of a scholar had once meant real-world authority alongside a religious turn of mind. Now the same garb—where preserved at all—was more like a symbol of otherworldly commitment. The point is not that religion was without inherent importance or respect, even in the secularizing Muslim world of the twentieth century. Rather, when compared to the confluence of religious and worldly power, the retreat to otherworldliness alone looked like a defeat. The source of this decline cannot be attributed wholly to a colonial worldview in which state authority trumped the religious authorities whom it preserved only to placate the population. After all, the Arab peoples had already *been* colonized by the Ottoman state, and for most of its history, that state had relied on the scholars' law both practically and as a source of legitimation.

That the new states that emerged in the aftermath of the Ottoman Empire did not rely upon the scholars and the shari'a for legitimation captures, more than anything else, how different the post-Ottoman constitutional order was from what came before it. When the scholars performed the institutional task of legitimation, the basis of legitimacy was that the ruler was acting to instantiate and apply the shari'a. Commanding good and forbidding evil was both the state's reason for being and the basis for the ruler's claim to be obeyed. It was in this sense that theorists of the classical Islamic constitution could assert that religion and political authority were twin brothers, each depending upon the other.[34]

In the post–World War I era, by contrast, the state jettisoned both its institutional reliance upon the scholars and its theoretical reliance upon the authority of the shari'a. This was, in constitutional terms, the end of the Islamic state. Subsequent states might pay homage to Islam, but to the extent that the state's ultimate authority was derived from the fact of sovereign power, not from the Islamic sources, those states merely recognized Islam and gave it a privileged place. They were not Islamic in the traditional sense.

At precisely the same time, the end of reliance on the scholars and the shari'a signified the birth of the constitutionally modern state in the Muslim world. Such states have the capacity to become rights-protecting and democratic, but modern non-liberal states have in common that the source of their legitimacy lies simply in the fact that they exercise power. It is true that the constitutional theory of the classical Islamic state did take account of power; but it did so within a rubric set by the shari'a, a rubric now abandoned by the new states of the Sunni Arab world.

It is possible, of course, to attribute the power-based form of the modern nonliberal state to colonialism, especially since the Ottoman sultan retained a claim to the caliphate to the bitter end. Certainly Western colonial powers brought with them their own theory of their right to rule, which was not based on any source of legitimacy located within Islam. But what undercuts this plausible colonial account and shifts the emphasis to the later Ottoman Empire is what happened in Turkey, the state that came to power in the Anatolian peninsula and represented all that remained of the once great empire.

Turkey did not come under colonial control after the war. Instead, the Young Turks who ultimately sought to displace the sultan took power, implementing what they took to be reforming advances that were relevant even now that Turkey was transforming itself into a nation-state within reduced borders. They developed a form of nationalism, familiar from European

86

models, in which the state's legitimacy derived precisely from the fact that it represented a coherent national group, namely, the Turks. The cosmopolitan Ottoman identity—any speaker of the Ottoman Turkish language could be an Ottoman, regardless of ethnicity—gave way to ethnic nationalism. (Not coincidentally, Arab nationalism was born in this same early twentieth-century milieu, arising to an important degree among Arabic-speakers educated in Istanbul and other Ottoman cities who were excluded from the nationalism of the Young Turks.)[35]

Eventually, one man, Kemal Pasha, known as Ataturk, consolidated authority in Turkey. In repressing religion, the shari'a, and the scholars, he went further than anyone had gone in thirteen centuries of Islamic civilization. His self-consciously Jacobin program of radical secularism all but severed the connection between state and religion, allowing the latter to exist only as a source of personal faith wholly subordinated to the state. After the empire collapsed, descendants of the sultan had continued to use the title caliph, offering a minimal and vestigial reminder of the old order. Ataturk put an end to the practice in 1924, formally abolishing the caliphate. It would be difficult to imagine a more definitive repudiation of the old Islamic constitutional order.

There is no question, of course, that Ataturk was emulating Western models of the modern, secular nation-state. What is important for our purposes is that he was able to accomplish this fundamental transformation without its being imposed by some Western power. Painful as were the changes that he forced upon Turkish society, the complete absence of any reliance on Islamic legitimacy—indeed, the opposite aspiration of relegating Islam to nothing but the backward faith of a few old people—showed that the scholars and their shari'a were already dead as meaningful sources of political legitimacy. To be sure, Ataturk's reforms were outward looking and European-oriented. But they nonetheless came from within Turkish society, not from outside. Ataturk went further than any other ruler in the Muslim world in marginalizing Islam (the one possible competitor being the Pahlavi shahs, to whom we shall return); but he resembled the other postwar leaders in his insistence upon total independence from the scholars and the shariʻa when it came to legitimating his rule.

Executive Dominance

If there is a single characteristic feature of the states that arose in the wake of the collapse of the Ottoman Empire over the course of the twentieth century, it is undoubtedly an unchecked executive dominating the rest of the government and, through it, society itself. In almost all cases, the first form of government following the empire was some sort of monarchy under foreign tutelage. Typically, though not exclusively, the monarchy failed and was replaced by a president or other strongman. The exemplar of this sort of government is Egypt, and the dictator-executive who set the mold was Gamal Abdel Nasser; but the model has applied to varying degrees in Syria, Iraq, Libya, Algeria, and Tunisia, to name just the most important examples. In a few cases—Morocco and Jordan—the monarchy survived, but only where it was successful in dominating the state and society in much the way that the presidents have done in the nonmonarchic states.

Why have these states—in particular the Arabic-speaking states of the former Ottoman Empire—been so susceptible in the last hundred years to executive dominance? Why have none of these states featured a powerful legislature or an effective, independent judiciary capable of counterbalancing the executive?[36] One possible answer to this question is that there is nothing special about these states in particular. The combination of standing armies and an apparatus of state intelligence has enabled quasi-military dictators to rule countries from Latin America to Africa to Asia. Local economic conditions and political cultures always differ, of course. As a result, the Latin American *caudillo* relies on different political symbols and rhetoric from those that characterize the Arab *ra'is*. But both, according to this view, are exemplars of executive power in its most potent and least limited form. It helps to have sources of revenue beyond taxes, whether in the form of oil or other mineral rents or in the form of direct payments from richer states around the world in search of allies. Even without these, however, a creative and charismatic leader may manage to keep his hands firmly on the helm of the ship of state, and to be removed only by his death, whether natural or unnatural.

No doubt there are some constant features of dictatorial executive power that can be identified across countries and political cultures. In every case, however, there will have to be some explanation of why political arrangements have become configured as they have. In most cases—certainly including many of those in Latin America and Africa—the legacy of colonialism assures that there will never have been any institutional model of balanced or divided government at the national level, except perhaps briefly and on paper at the moment of liberation from colonial rule. Neither will the rule of law have been much respected in the history of most such countries.

If the period of British and French colonialism in the Arab world is taken as the starting point of our analysis, then the same observation could be extended to states like Iraq or Syria, which never had effective counterbalances to executive power in the modern period. If, however, we direct our historical lens a little further, we will be able to observe that in the Ottoman era and before, these places came within the orbit of a constitutional order in which balanced powers were the norm and something very like the rule of law prevailed. The same could not be said of Latin America under Spanish rule (or before), or of most sub-Saharan African states under the various colonial regimes that existed in them (or before).

Given the classical Islamic constitutional system of balanced powers and the rule of law, why has this system failed to renew itself in the modern states of the Arabic-speaking world? The answer, I want to propose, reflects the fact that the displacement of the shari'a and the decline of the scholarly class left behind no institutional force capable of effectuating a replacement. In such an environment, there is no obvious barrier to the growth of the unchecked executive. The public inevitably will be dissatisfied with unchecked executive power, especially when it fails to deliver on presidential promises. Yet this generalized dissatisfaction lacks any institutional rallying point that would enable the opposition to organize itself into a viable alternative.

It follows from this analysis that the nature of unchecked presidentialism in the Arab world is distinctive. It derives in particular from the abandonment of the only constitutional order in the public's collective memory that was able to deliver what looked like justice: the rule of the shari'a, assured by a constitutional balance of powers. With the loss of the shari'a as a basis for state legitimacy, and the decline of the class whose historical role had always been to maintain constitutional legitimacy, a range of Arabic-speaking societies lost the collective imaginative capability of substantial organized resistance to the power of the state.

The point is *not* that Arab or Islamic political norms are distinctively obedient, as is sometimes asserted, or uniquely oriented toward recognition of power or force. Centuries of government through law, legitimated by law, betray this cultural analysis. Nor is it plausible to think that Islamic political culture is making the judgment, sometimes attributed to it on the basis of a proverb, that sixty years of tyranny are better than a day of anarchy.[37] The meaning of this adage is not that tyranny is to be suffered lightly, but rather that even a small amount of anarchy is far more disastrous and far-reaching than would otherwise be assumed. (Iraq during the U.S. occupation is a good example of this observation's power.)

Rather, what marks the failure of institutions and society in many Muslim and especially Arab countries to resist executive tyranny is the experience of losing the class of persons whose job it was for centuries to offer a site for that resistance. Legitimation, as I argued in Part I, implies delegitimation. The shari'a provided a theory of what the state was for; and also, by implication, what the state was not designed to do. Its disappearance from the discourse of political legitimacy devastated the capacity of Arab countries to resist unchecked autocratic authority. This helps explain why there has been so little in the way of energized rule-of-law or democracy movements in most Arab states (Lebanon in recent years is the exception).

The only rallying cry that has managed to achieve some degree of staying power in the Arabic-speaking countries is the claim that the presidential governments in power have abandoned the teachings of Islam. It will be the topic of Part III to attempt to show how the phenomenon of political Islamism may be understood in terms of the aspiration to a constitutional order grounded in the shari'a and devoted to the rule of law. For now, it is enough to observe that the Islamists' language and theory of resistance to autocratic executive power does not come from nowhere, but springs from identifiable beliefs and ideals about what politics ought to be.

The Saudi Exception

One unique case in the Arabic-speaking world represents the exception that must be used to test the general theory of constitutional collapse that I have been sketching. That is the case of Saudi Arabia, one of the only countries in the whole of the Muslim world that preserves some recognizable version of the classical Islamic constitutional order—and the one Arab country where executive power is today counterbalanced by the scholars.

The point, of course, is not to claim that the Sunni Muslim world would have been better off had it preserved this classical order. Saudi Arabia is in no sense a model for others to emulate. It is not on the road to Western democracy, and it is far from clear that it is even tending toward constitutional monarchy. The reason this is so, I want to argue, is that the classical constitutional order was ill-prepared to cope with the infusion of oil revenue that enabled the Saudi state to dominate society in unprecedented ways. Furthermore, the Saudi example is powerfully influenced by the distinctive values held by the Saudi scholars, which differ in certain crucial respects from the more mainstream views of scholars throughout Islamic history. Nevertheless, the Saudi case does show how balanced constitutional powers can operate in the contemporary Muslim world—and how they render Saudi Arabia substantially different from other Arabic-speaking states.

The place to begin is with Saudi Arabia's anomalous history.[38] Ottoman rule in Arabia extended only along the Western coast of the peninsula, including the province of Hijaz, where Mecca and Medina are located. It did not, however, include the interior of the country or the east coast, which was governed for much of the eighteenth and nineteenth centuries by what are called the first and second Saudi states. These protostates, autonomous entities based in the central Arabian plateau, known as the Najd, withstood outside pressures primarily because it was not worthwhile for the Ottoman sultan or indeed anybody else to conquer the area. The Ottomans barely bothered to intervene in Saudi business, except, for example, in 1802, when the first Saudi state humiliated the empire by venturing forth from the plateau and conquering Mecca and Medina. The Ottoman sultan, as caliph and keeper of the holy places, had little choice but to retaliate, and he eventually sent an army that by 1818 defeated the Saudi state and exiled its leadership. The sultan even had the prince of the Saudi state executed in Istanbul. Within a few years, though, the second Saudi state had replaced the first, this time limiting its rule to the plateau and hence remaining unmolested by the empire until its defeat in 1891 by a local tribal rival.

The two Saudi states were not fully states in the modern sense, lacking most of the bureaucratic apparatus we associate with the term, and barely aspiring to monopolize legitimate violence. They had their origin in 1744 through the alliance of two great men: Muhammad Ibn Saʿud, the founder of the dynasty, and Shaykh Muhammad Ibn ʿAbd al-Wahhab, one of most influential religious leaders in modern Islamic history. The relation between these two men set much of the course of future Saudi history.

Muhammad Ibn Saʿud was an effective tribal military leader, skilled in the art of the raid, and advanced in his interest in conquest rather than merely plunder. Yet he would have remained an obscure figure were it not for his genius in allying his cause with Ibn ʿAbd al-Wahhab's movement for religious reform. Ibn ʿAbd al-Wahhab sought to purify Islam from what he considered the mistaken accretions of custom and culture, and to return it to the pure, refined faith and practice that he attributed to the Prophet Muhammad. Those who opposed his interpretation were enemies and even heretics. They included Shi'is, whom he considered beyond the pale, but also orthodox Sunnis who engaged in customary practices like Sufi mysticism, the veneration of holy men, or the visiting of the tombs of their illustrious ancestors. To engage in such practices was to substitute external things for the one divine truth. Even celebrating the birthday of the Prophet, an ancient tradition, ran the risk of substituting worship of the Prophet for worship of God. Under Muhammad Ibn Sa'ud's leadership, tombs were sacked and customs suppressed in the name of God's unity.

As it turned out, this reform impulse came to provide a unifying and legitimating authority to the force of the protostate that was giving it life. Instead of underwriting merely a series of short-term captures and short-lived reforms, the potent combination of Wahhabism and Saudi force was able to establish lasting government. When Ibn 'Abd al-Wahhab and Muhammad Ibn Sa'ud died, each left behind a family line eager to continue its distinctive role in this partnership of scholars and princes. The charisma of the two men was transformed into a distinctive institutionalized relationship. The relationship between the House of Sa'ud and the House of the Shaykh (as Ibn 'Abd al-Wahhab's family was called) survived both Saudi states, eventually becoming the legitimating force behind the modern Saudi state.

The modern Saudi state is usually dated to 1902, when 'Abd al-'Aziz Ibn Sa'ud recaptured Riyadh and reestablished control over the central plateau. This Ibn Sa'ud, destined to become better known than his predecessor Muhammad Ibn Sa'ud, stepped onto the global stage in 1925, when he conquered the western province of Hijaz, including the cities of Mecca and Medina, defeating King Husayn ibn 'Ali.

Unlike Ibn Sa'ud at the time, King Husayn was already world-famous—as sharif of Mecca, he had led the Arab Revolt that had been promoted (and exploited) by T. E. Lawrence. An established presence in international circles, Husayn had earned British friendship through his efforts against the Ottomans in World War I. In recompense, the British had given his family the monarchies of Iraq, Syria, Hijaz, and Transjordan after the defeat of the Ottomans. Two days after Ataturk put an end to the caliphate in Istanbul in 1924, Husayn had himself declared caliph with authority over the whole of the Muslim world. Within a couple of years, defeated by Ibn Saʿud, Husayn was not even lord of the Hijaz.

Thus, even though the modern Saudi state encompassed symbolically crucial territory formerly under the control of the Ottoman Empire, the Saudi state was unique in not inheriting political norms from that empire. It also was never subject to foreign tutelage equivalent to colonization. This history, combined with the legacy of the close relationship between the executive and the scholars in the earlier Saudi states, gave rise to a form of government very different from what has obtained elsewhere in the region.[39]

For one thing, from its inception until today, the Saudi state has never adopted a written constitution. This is a marker of similarity to the classical Islamic constitutional order, in which no written constitution was necessary to specify that the formal authority of the state derived from its implementation of the shariʿa as interpreted by the scholars. In Saudi Arabia, it is the scholars who have consistently opposed any written constitution, which, they realize, could only reduce their importance. Even if such a document purported simply to declare that the shariʿa was the ultimate authority, the act of declaration could imply that such a declaration was necessary, and in this way would undercut the background assumption of the primacy of divine Law.[40]

For another thing, although the Saudi king has never declared himself to be caliph, the basis for his authority is understood by one and all to be his fulfillment of the obligation to command the good and forbid the wrong as defined by the shariʻa. From this it follows that the king lacks the authority to legislate—and it goes without saying that no other legislative body exists, either. Law, properly speaking, is what the scholars, using the interpretive process, understand God to have commanded. Administrative regulations may, of course, be issued by the king, as they always were during the course of Islamic constitutional history. To the extent that Saudi Arabia has codified "laws," they consist in royal regulations that do not contradict or supersede the shariʻa. But the shariʻa itself in Saudi Arabia is not codified—and under the constitutional arrangement as it presently exists, it could not be codified without displacing the scholars from their proper place.

The scholarly class in Saudi Arabia is, formally speaking, independent of the state. Although patronage facilitated by oil revenues has in important ways compromised this independence, in principle the scholars as a group are not employed or controlled by the government. Entrance into the community of scholars is based upon scholarly qualification, which is itself regulated not solely by the granting of degrees from state-sponsored educational institutions but on the informal judgment of the scholarly community and the granting of formal permission by more senior muftis to issue fatwas. Although the Saudi state does recognize the office of grand mufti, the state is to a meaningful degree constrained by scholarly reputation when appointing a scholar to this post. What is more, the grand mufti does not have more authority than any other mufti with respect to the binding character of his fatwas. Judges in Saudi Arabia are drawn from among qualified scholars, assuring another traditional mechanism for the scholars' maintenance of control over the substance of the law. The traditional skepticism within the scholarly class about judicial service is also remembered, though it is possible to say that it is respected more in the breach, since government service provides a degree of remuneration that would have been unimaginable before the influx of oil revenue.

Most important for consolidation of the scholars' position in the constitutional order is that they maintain an identity as keepers of the shari'a and as the class of persons with the appropriate authority to confer legitimacy upon the state—or to withhold it. Important policy decisions made by the state apparatus require justification by fatwa. Perhaps the most famous case of such a fatwa was the one issued by a committee including the late grand mufti 'Abd al-'Aziz bin Baz, authorizing the deployment of American troops on Saudi soil during the U.S. war to force Saddam Hussein out of Kuwait in 1991. This fatwa has become well known for the ironic reason that Osama bin Laden challenged it frontally in the first major public pronouncement of his career.[41] Taken on its own terms, however, the fatwa reflected the ruler's sense that even fundamental decisions concerning national security needed validation by the scholarly authorities if they were not to detract from the state's legitimacy.

Other salient examples of the power of the scholars may be seen on domestic policy issues that, according to the scholars, implicate the shari'a. Ibn Sa'ud himself sought formal permission from the scholars to introduce wireless into the kingdom, such a means of communication obviously not having existed at the time of the Prophet.[42] More recently, the scholars have effectively and intensively resisted the granting of permission to women to drive cars in Saudi Arabia[43]—an issue that has caused substantial external embarrassment to the government, and which the ruler would presumably be eager to make disappear, were it not for the apparent impossibility of inducing sufficient consent from the scholarly community.

In certain ways, in fact, the position of the ruler vis-à-vis the scholars in the contemporary Saudi Arabia may be weaker than was the position of the ruler of the classical Islamic state in relation to the scholars with whom he had to deal. The House of the Shaykh was not simply a post hoc legitimator but part of the very force that brought the House of Sa'ud into power in the first place. The Saudi scholars are more than scholars; they are active, quasi-tribal allies of the Sa'ud family. In some nontrivial way, then, the Saudi scholars are actually part of the ruling class. If it is sometimes said that the Saudi royal family with its seven thousand princes must be thought of as a kind of political party, then the Saudi scholars may arguably be seen as an adjunct to that party—a special department of intellectuals and propagandists devoted to maintaining their own position through the act of sustaining the Saudi state.

And what a state it is. As if the history of Ibn Sa'ud and his progeny were not distinctive and unusual enough, Saudi Arabia is also anomalous in being home to the world's largest proven oil reserves.[44] To be sure, Ibn Sa'ud did not seek dominance on the Arabian Peninsula in order to control the oil. Like the first rulers of the other Gulf principalities, who also now share in the oil riches of the region, Ibn Sa'ud conquered for reasons of his own and without knowing just what extraordinary wealth the conquest would eventually reap. Over the course of the twentieth century, however, as more and more cheaply accessible oil was discovered, and as oil became increasingly necessary to the rapidly growing global economy, the Saudi state was able to generate per capita revenues on a truly extraordinary scale. Moreover, unlike some countries, such as the United States, where the earliest oil magnates were private individuals like the

Rockefellers, in Saudi Arabia the oil always and only belonged to the state treasury.

Although the Saʿud family has spent freely on its own creature comforts, a very substantial share of the state's very substantial revenues has been spent on consolidating the power of the Saudi state. Its expenditures go well beyond infrastructure. They include the establishment of a wide range of institutional structures, funded either by the government directly or by individual members of the royal family, which collectively employ large swaths of Saudi society. Of course such a structure, combining government with the economy and society, is susceptible to the fluctuations of the price of oil on the international markets. When the price of oil dips, the crunch is felt by everybody who relies on direct or indirect state funding. When the price of oil goes up, though, the Saudi state exercises an influence over the daily workings of Saudi society that is possibly unmatched in any state in the world.

The scholarly class is by no means immune from this influence. Scholars working in official government posts receive salaries, as they always have throughout Islamic constitutional history; scholars who are nominally outside government, though, also receive subventions in the form of salary from academic institutions that are in effect state controlled. At any moment, the state can elevate the wealth of any given scholar to previously unimagined levels. By the same token, the state may, exercising caution, demote or even imprison scholars whose views deviate too widely from the favored line.

One might have thought that the state's extraordinary power to create economic and other incentives for the scholarly class would have enabled it to swallow up the independent role traditionally played by those scholars under the Saudi version of the classical Islamic constitution. Some critics of the Saudi scholarly class—Osama bin Laden among them—have argued just this, insisting that the occasional moderate ruling from the grand mufti or his associates reflects their lack of independence from state influence. Yet the claim goes too far. In many instances, the Saudi state would be happy to minimize or at least reduce the influence of the scholars. But the practice of buying off the scholars turns out to be a more subtle and complicated one than might at first appear. The scholars in Saudi Arabia are in some way participants in the state apparatus, making it difficult for "the state" to marginalize them; and the legitimacy of the monarchy is so deeply bound up in its historical ties to the scholars that their co-optation must be undertaken gingerly.

Where the Saudi constitutional order differs most fundamentally from the classical order is not in the bilateral relation between the ruler and the scholars, but in the triangular relationship interconnecting the rulers, the scholars, and the ruled. In the classical order, I argued earlier, the necessity of taxation was one of the main reasons why the rulers needed to establish and maintain their legitimacy. In the Saudi oil monarchy, however, taxation—at least of ordinary citizens—is irrelevant to the capacity of the state to raise the revenues it needs to operate. Instead of gathering revenues from the citizens in order to finance public goods, the state may simply rely on the bounty of the oil resources.[45]

As a result, the state does not need to maintain the kind of relationship with its citizens in which they would be prepared to open their pocketbooks and transfer their hard-earned money to a government that would owe them services in return. In a state where revenues derive not from the citizens' wealth but from the state's independent asset base, most citizens will be prepared to accept whatever government they have unless some much better option presents itself. For that to happen, either the present government must be so oppressive that another option begins to look desirable, or else some extraneous ideological force must be so powerful as to impugn, in the minds of citizens, the government's legitimate right to rule.[46]

The key to understanding the constitutional structure of the Saudi state in contradistinction to that of the classical Islamic state is that the oil wealth greatly reduces the rulers' worry that popular unrest might lead to a coup d'état or revolution. That does not mean the rulers are utterly confident that they could not be displaced, especially by other members of the royal family. As in the classical Islamic constitutional arrangement, the scholars must be kept on board precisely so that they do not support, either explicitly or implicitly, efforts by other pretenders to the throne. But the popular legitimacy that the ruler needs, and that the scholars traditionally helped the ruler to maintain, is simply much less significant in a state that dispenses wealth to its citizens rather than gathering it from them in the form of taxes.

It emerges, therefore, that the scholars' capacity to protect the rule of law in the contemporary Saudi state is much weaker than it was in the classical Islamic state. The difference is that the scholars are far less useful to the rulers than they would be in a state without overwhelming oil wealth. The scholars remain meaningful players in the Saudi constitutional order—much more meaningful, indeed, than in any other currently existing Sunni state. They maintain quasi-independence despite the state's extraordinary ability to buy them off, largely on account of their distinctive historical role as near equal partners in the definition of the state's legitimacy and reason for being. But because popular legitimacy is largely unnecessary, the scholars' traditional ability to help deliver it carries less influence than it would have done absent the distorting effects of oil wealth.

101

Relative to the classical Islamic constitution, the Saudi constitutional order is an image in a distorted looking glass. All the familiar elements are there, but their size, their placement, and their interrelationship are altered and affected by oil. In this sense, Saudi Arabia reveals not the constitutional order that might have been, but rather what happens when traditional constitutional structures persist under radically new conditions instead of being replaced by new structures better suited to the modern era.

III

THE RISE OF THE NEW
ISLAMIC STATE

Islamism as a Modernist Ideology

IT IS AN EXTRAORDINARY fact about the fall of the classical Islamic state that the scholars, its greatest advocates and the interest group with the most to lose by its destruction, did not put up the kind of fight that might have drawn notice to the constitutional disaster that was to follow. Equally remarkable is the fact that the call for the return to an Islamic state has not, with the important and telling exception of the Shiʻi world, been led by scholars calling for the restoration of the old order and their place in it. Instead, in the Sunni Muslim world, the call for the creation of a new Islamic state governed by Islamic law has come from the political-religious movement known as Islamism. The most influential mainstream Islamist organization, the transnational Muslim Brotherhood, was founded in Egypt in 1928; today Islamist movements of various stripes are major players from Morocco and Algeria through Palestine, Jordan, Lebanon, and the Gulf, all the way to Afghanistan, Pakistan, and even Southeast Asia. The most important figures in Islamism in the modern era have almost never been trained scholars. For the most part, they have been Muslims educated in the Western arts and especially sciences[1] who have found in Islam a language to express profound frustration with the political order and a powerfully resonant vision of how that order ought to be reformed.

Why have the Sunni scholars not mounted a substantial or sustained movement for an Islamic state, especially when, as we shall see, their Shi'i contemporaries have not only called for an Islamic state but have actually created one in Iran? To answer this question it is useful to consider the crucial way in which the constitutional vision of modern Islam*ism* differs from that of classical Islam. The classical Islamic constitutional order grew out of the development and interplay of institutions that had a basis in familiar, traditional, and customary ways of life and governance. Its structures were organic, and their relationship to the state symbiotic.

The constitutional proposals of Islamism, by contrast, are products of twentieth-century ideology in its most distinctive sense. Like communism, socialism, and nationalism, Islamism as a movement seeks to capture the reins of the existing state and then to transform society through a program of principles and laws capable of being implemented by decree. As an ideological movement, Islamism boasts of its capacity to create something new and pure—the fulfillment of an abstract ideal whose content may be found in written books, not in the collective wisdom and knowledge of a particular social class. And like the other prominent ideologies of the twentieth century, Islamism is fiercely egalitarian.[2]

The impulse to treat all people—or at least all men—as equals in the creation of the new political order sits uneasily with the notion of the scholars as a distinctive class of trained professionals possessing unique access to the content of the divine will expressed in law. This helps explain both why Islamism has not sought the restoration of the scholars to their traditional position as part of its constitutional program and also why the scholars themselves—outside the Shi'i world—have never effectively sought that restoration. Once the incorporation of law into the state deprived the scholars of their role as keepers of the legal order, their distinctive claim to elevated status—specialized knowledge of the Islamic legal tradition—

disappeared with it. Taking away the chief domain of scholarship made the scholars appear almost purposeless, leaving them with little to administer save matters of personal piety. Their reason for significance gone, the scholars gave way to the press of equality that has played such a crucial role on every continent in the history of the twentieth century.

Adding insult to injury, the scholars' limited jurisdiction in the area of family law made them seem irrelevant to the broader political order. They were not only functionaries; they were functionaries who served the government in what was perceived as the relatively unimportant personal sphere. In this reduced condition, the Sunni scholars ceased to be a political constituency around which a political movement could be organized. And from the standpoint of the Islamists, the scholars appeared no longer necessary for the interpretation and application of Islamic law.

The early Islamists—men like Hassan al-Banna, the founder of the Muslim Brotherhood, and Sayyid Qutb, Islamism's most radical and arguably most influential theorist—were motivated in large part by the apparent collapse of the Islamic order in the period after World War I. They wanted first and foremost to restore Islamic society to its rightful place in the world. Because they diagnosed the failure of Islamic society to have been caused by the abandonment of religion itself, they sought to return Islam to a central life-role *in order to improve the overall condition of Muslim society.*

For the Islamists, Islam was put into the service of a broader project of societal restoration and repair. The Muslim Brotherhood was from its start designed not simply or even primarily as a religious association, but rather as a comprehensive organization, encompassing social, political, educational, and even athletic activities.[3] In this respect, the Brotherhood both imitated and went beyond the traditional Sufi brotherhood, a religious organization with fraternal features. Social solidarity was a feature of each; but self-consciously organizing a group for the uplift of its membership and of society as a whole was the distinctively modern project of the Muslim Brotherhood.

The Islamists, then, saw Islam as a social-political tool suitable to the modern age. Yet the traditional texts of Islamic law and theology did not depict it in that way. Neither did the scholars conceptualize Islam in such instrumental or forward-looking terms. The solution of the Islamists was to look back, before the development of the "religious sciences" in which the scholars specialized, straight to the great and inspiring source: the Qur'an itself.

The return to the Qur'an as a touchstone of true Islam resonated to some degree with the reformist tradition in Islam, according to which every several generations a person or movement might emerge to "renew" Islam by freeing it of unnecessary accretions and superstitions. Muhammad Ibn 'Abd al-Wahhab, whom we met in Part II, is a good example of this paradigm. And there were indeed some parallels between Islamism and Wahhabism, sufficient for the Saudi government at various times in the last century to have offered its active support to certain Islamists despite the profound differences between their respective worldviews. At the same time, although the Islamists would not acknowledge the influence, Islamism's turn to the Qur'an bore a certain similarity to Protestantism—especially the doctrine of "scripture alone," and the rejection of canonical interpretations of law and theology that the Roman Catholic Church had developed over centuries.[4]

Over the last century, Islamists have been prepared to circumvent, and even implicitly repudiate, certain aspects of the tradition that intervened between the Prophet and the modern era. Specifically, for political-programmatic reasons, Islamists have wanted to do away with the scholars' monopoly on the shari'a and its institutions. This willingness reflects a very basic difference between the Islamists and more tradition-minded movements like Saudi-inspired salafism, which hews much more closely to its own strand of the Islamic legal tradition Nonscholars themselves, the Islamists by contrast seek a world in which nonscholars run the state in accordance with values derived from Islam. The necessary precondition of this ideal is to imagine that there exist Islamic values and ideals that can be identified and applied without reliance on the scholars.

To do so, the Islamists rely on the notion that the individual may interpret the Qur'an on his own, even against the authority of the scholars. Islam, unlike Catholicism, never formally restricted scriptural interpretation to the scholarly class. But in practice, access was limited by the extensive education in the religious sciences that was necessary for an individual to become conversant in the tradition of interpretation. In the case of legal interpretation, the issuance of formal opinions *was* restricted to authorized muftis.

The Islamists have set out to reverse this; and it is fair to say that they have had considerable success in this regard. There is a range of opinion within the Islamist camp on this issue, with more liberal Islamists prepared to amend the teachings of the scholars even on family law matters, and more conservative Islamists still preserving a role for the scholars in the limited jurisdiction of ritual matters. In general, however, although Sunni Islamists respect scholars personally, the great majority of them believe that the Islamic values that direct the state's behavior need not be mapped out by scholars or even derived narrowly from the classical scholarly tradition. Instead, the ordinary believer may search the text of the Qur'an and the most authoritative hadith traditions with the goal of interpreting them to identify principles of Islam that may be applied to state behavior—including even the legal decisions of the state.

In practice, this has meant that when Islamists call for the shari'a—as they invariably do—they are not calling for the restoration of the full classical Islamic legal system under the guidance of the scholars who traditionally shaped and controlled that system. The Islamists' political platforms do, crucially, call for the *rule* of the shari'a—indeed, this is their most distinctive and remarkable feature.[5] They do not, however, call for the creation of an Islamic legal system peopled by trained scholars who would take over the administration of justice. Notwithstanding the prominence of some contemporary scholars in the role of spiritual advisers to the Muslim Brotherhood, according to the Islamists, the basic institutional jobs in the modern state—the executive, legislative, judicial, and bureaucratic functions—are to be filled by state-appointed nonscholars.

The Islamists' model, in other words, could not be further from the restoration of the scholars to their traditional constitutional position. It is, in fact, premised on the *replacement* of these scholars by ordinary Muslim laymen who must be guided by their own, nonscholarly interpretation of Islamic tradition. While the Islamists typically seek to people all parts of the government with sympathetic, Islamist-oriented personnel in order to advance their own particular version of Islamic values, it has in general not been the practice of Sunni Islamists to seek the appointment of scholars to such positions. This approach is reflected by polls reporting that the Muslim public—despite its broad embrace of a major role for the shari'a in government—does not want religious leaders to govern directly, preferring some sort of "advisory" role for the scholars.[6]

It might be thought that Islamists refrain from seeking the appointment of scholars to government posts simply because this would be seen as too radical a challenge to the existing quasi-secular constitutional arrangements in most Muslim countries. In some outlying cases, like Afghanistan, where for decades what little educational system existed was entirely Islamic, Islamists have made efforts to get scholars into at least some government posts. But this exception proves the rule. Just about everywhere else, the Islamists represent a class distinct from the waning scholars, with different education and different interests. The Islamists envision government run by them, according to the shari'a and Islamic values as they define and apply them—which is to say, with very limited scholarly input.[7] As a result, their shari'a-oriented constitutional proposal represents not the classical Islamic constitution but something very different: a novel set of Islamized constitutional arrangements. To see this, we shall now turn to the more comprehensive versions of the Islamist political platform.

Islamist Shari'a and Islamic Shari'a: The Question of Justice

The Islamist political program always calls for the establishment of an "Islamic" state, with the word "Islam" used in its modern adjectival meaning—a sense largely absent from the classical vocabulary.[8] "Islam," understood as an encompassing and modern ideology, is therefore definitionally the crucial element of Islamism. Islam, according to this view, is the thing that makes Islamism into a distinctive approach to the reform of government and society. It is the engine meant to restore Muslim societies to world prominence and power.[9]

When called upon to define the Islamic character of the state as they envision it, Islamists typically say that what makes the state Islamic is that it is governed through Islamic law and Islamic values.[10] The legal part of this definition is, at least in

Ibn
Taymiya

theory, influenced by history. As we have seen, Islamic law was the central defining feature of the classical Islamic constitutional order, a fact recognized by the Islamists. So an Islamic state must be under Islamic law, however its form may have been transmuted by codification. To speak of an Islamic state without a central role for Islamic law would call into question the very category "Islamic."

The second element of the definition, which speaks of Islamic "values," has a subtly different status. Islamic "values," or as Qutb had it, "the spirit of Islam," is not a concept that can be found in the classical Islamic literature, whether constitutional or otherwise. There is a category known to classical religious-political thought as "shariʿa politics" (*siyasa sharʿi-yya*).[11] But even this locution, closely associated with the scholar Ibn Taymiya, discussed in Part I, relates politics to Islamic law, rather than connecting Islam itself with the amorphous category of "values." To define the Islamic state as one that adopts Islamic values is therefore to embrace a distinctively modern vision of the state, one that frees the state from the narrow bounds of classical Islamic legality. This room for maneuver turns out to be crucial to the Islamist project.

For reasons that deserve close attention, Islamism has a very difficult and fraught relationship with the notion of Islamic law. In political terms, Islamic law is both an important selling point for the Islamists and also a potential threat to their ability to take and wield power in the modern world. On the positive side, Islamism's appeal to its potential supporters depends in part on the perception that, after the abandonment of Islamic law, Muslim societies collapsed under the weight of unbridled executive power. By invoking the Islamic state governed by the shariʿa, the Islamists tap into the nostalgic and in many ways accurate idea that the classical Islamic state was just—or at least much more just than the autocratic states that the modern era

112

has brought to most majority-Muslim countries. Calling for a return to Islamic law conjures the possibility of repairing the political corruption of the past century and returning to a purer order in which the shari'a governed social and governmental relations.

In order to capture these positive associations with the legal order of the classical Islamic state, the political language of contemporary Islamists is dominated by the term "justice." It is tricky but nonetheless important to pin down the notion of justice that the Islamists are using. Certainly the word is a kind of leitmotif for the movement, understood to signal Islamism in most of the Arabic-speaking world. Numerous Islamist political parties incorporate it into their names; and if the term has sometimes been adopted because the government will not allow the word "Islam" into the name of a political party, that simply underscores the fact that "justice" is the euphemism of choice for Islam.[12]

We might distinguish three different kinds of justice that are intertwined in this usage: social justice, political justice, and legal justice. The first of these terms has an important legacy in Islamist thought, dating to the publication of Qutb's 1949 classic *Social Justice in Islam*.[13] Although the book of Qutb's that has received most Western attention recently is his much more radical *Milestones*[14]—a key text in the emergence of radically violent jihadism—the earlier work is a more important text for mainstream Islamism and its political-constitutional platform.

For Qutb, the category of the social was significant for its rejection of what he considered a Western dichotomy between religion and society. In the book, social justice incorporates economic, personal, and governmental relations, including—without much specificity—the legal system. Qutb seeks to chart a middle path between socialism and capitalism, emphasizing equality of opportunity rather than equality of outcomes, and mild redistribution of wealth through a tax system inspired by the classical Islamic taxes. He also speaks in general terms about eliminating oppression and facilitating equal citizenship without hierarchy, including clerical hierarchy. But Qutb does not, in the work, sketch the specific political or constitutional structures that Islam requires. The word "social" may have been intended in part to placate the government censor by avoiding an overt call for fundamental *political* change.

Whatever Qutb's caution, however, political justice is indeed crucial to the Islamists' justice-based platform and has been since before Qutb's time. The key element of the Islamists' picture of political justice is certainly an end to unjust government. The Middle East's oppressive or dictatorial regimes, generally secular, are depicted in Islamist literature as tyrannical. (Or, in a metaphor drawn from the Qur'an and especially trenchant in Egypt, as pharaonic.) Although the Islamists do not always call for the use of force to achieve this goal, they also do not shrink from it. The Muslim Brotherhood presents itself as peaceful, and its affiliates regularly take part in elections;[15] but it also supports Hamas, itself a Brotherhood offshoot. Muslim Brothers were accused of attempting to assassinate Gamal Abdel Nasser, and a radical Islamist group did manage to assassinate his successor, Anwar Sadat.

But beyond deposing tyrants, the Islamist model of political justice also involves the establishment of benign governments that are responsible to the principles of the shari'a as described by the Islamists. This image implies the existence of governing institutions, to which we shall turn in a moment. These are imagined as honest, fair, not corrupt, and indeed incorruptible.

Closely associated with this ideal of political justice is the implicit invocation by the Islamists of legal justice. The shari'a does enormous work in this context, since by calling for government by shari'a the Islamists are not, as noted above, demanding a return to the classical Islamic state with its qadis, muftis, and supplemental administrative regulations. Instead, the Islamists are evoking the image of a just legal system, one that administers the law fairly—without bias, corruption by the rich, or government interference. One might even say that the "justice" of the Islamists' discourse is primarily legal justice, insofar as the shari'a is often the most specific substantive plank of the Islamist platform, thought capable of subsuming the rest.[16]

Strengthening the legal justice component of the Islamists' justice is the fact that the word "justice" is not simply an abstract noun in Arabic. It is also a particular legal term, drawn from the jurisprudential literature, which describes a quality or trait of being law-abiding that may be possessed by an individual who is then qualified to give reliable testimony or perform certain public functions.[17] By association, speaking of justice also suggests the honesty and incorruptibility of the Islamist politicians—who, on the whole, have indeed been less corrupt than the officials of secular majority-Muslim states.

The negative political side of the invocation of the shari'a is that, taken as a set of substantive rules, the classical Islamic law is decidedly nonmodern. As we saw in Part II, a modernizing Ottoman Empire found it had to supplement and modify classical Islamic laws in order to keep up with the times, and with the important exception of Saudi Arabia (which has also been forced to adopt extensive supplemental administrative regulations), almost no contemporary majority-Muslim state purports to apply it exclusively. That means the Muslim public understands that a return to the shari'a, if actually attempted, would entail the substantial challenge of updating old ways to new circumstances.

115

To exacerbate matters, in the Muslim world as in the West, the nonmodern features of the shari'a that are most salient include harsh corporal punishments. These are not necessarily popular practices among Muslims, and in any case appear decidedly premodern to most observers. The Islamists therefore face real political risk when they make Islamic law into a centerpiece of their political platform. They are able to take the high ground with respect to the crucial issues of anticorruption and the rule of law, but at the same time, they place themselves in the position of strict enforcers of measures that are unlikely to be popular. They also incur the wrath and fear of Western critics, whether drawn from the international human rights community or from the ranks of neoliberals who see reversion to a premodern legal system as economically and politically undesirable. That the Islamists nevertheless retain this element in their program is a testimony to how heavily they weigh their commitment to the rule of law.

The other great difficulty associated with the reliance on Islamic law in the Islamist program is the problem it introduces with respect to the scholars. Historically, what made Islamic government distinctive was a constitutional order in which the implementation of the shari'a was the nominal raison d'être of the state and the prime way of legitimating its use of force. Islamic law, understood to comprehend both the classical constitutional order and the legal order that obtained under it, structured private legal relations as well as relations between state and citizen.

Yet Islamism, as its advocates seek to implement it, denies a central or distinctive role to the scholarly class that traditionally gave life to the Islamic character of the state. For reasons that, we have seen, lie in its impulses to modernity and egalitarianism, Islamism denies the scholars their traditionally dominant

116

role in the exercise of legal power. Under Islamist principles, the scholars are not envisioned as the keepers of Islam or as the ultimate arbiters of Islamic values. The colonial and late-Ottoman tendency to relegate the scholars to the role of family-court judges is essentially maintained in the Islamist picture of government.

Given that Islamic law is, historically speaking, the product of the scholarly community, how can Islamic law be said to rule when it is not to be shaped or controlled by the scholars who were its keepers? The answer is a paradox: shari'a without the scholars. In this way, the Islamic state envisioned by the Islamists could not be more different from the Islamic state of the classical constitutional order. The old Islamic state was rendered Islamic by the scholars and on their account. The new Islamic state is Islamic despite the scholars' absence from its institutions.

The Democratization of the Shari'a?

Islamism, then, calls for the shari'a and its justice but without conferring authority over the law on the scholars who were long its keepers. What would be the shape and administration of Islamic law without the active institutional participation of the scholarly class? One possible answer lies in the notion of Islamic law as a new kind of legislation. Enacted and applied by nonscholars, it would nonetheless comprise the true spirit and content of the divine will made into contemporary law.

The Ottoman legal codes offer one version of Islamic law as substantively Islamic legislation. Bodies of statute law based upon one or more schools of classical jurisprudence could be administered by judges without specific scholarly training. This

117

model was followed to a certain degree by those modern Arab states that adopted versions of Sanhuri's codes. These codes were themselves drafted in the light of civil law norms that Sanhuri occasionally modified to reflect Islamic legal rules. They, too, could be administered by judges without Islamic legal training, and they were in spirit hybridized and selectively Islamic.

It is notable that both of these models for the adoption of Islamic statutory legislation were produced by specialist drafters who possessed considerable expertise in the substance of Islamic law. The disadvantage of this mode of lawmaking consists in the way that it fails to account adequately for the divine origin and authority of the law itself. In the self-accounting of classical Islamic law, the scholars were assigned the task of interpreting God's will as expressed through the prophecy and example of Muhammad. The authority to engage in this interpretation came from the very tradition being interpreted, and the state accepted its obligation to apply the law as the scholars understood it. The result was a coherent legal-constitutional theory that established the legitimacy of both law and state by reference to the divine.

The Islamists would also like to acknowledge what they refer to as God's "sovereignty." But without the scholars to fulfill the role of authorized interpreters of God's law, the Islamists find themselves in difficulties when they try to explain how and why Islamic law should govern. For most of the last century, Islamist literature has basically avoided dealing with the issue. It presents Islamic law as a promising source for social salvation, with no serious attempt made to explain, constitutionally or theologically, what would justify its adoption and implementation. The fact that Islamists have very rarely achieved actual power in the Sunni world has reduced their burden of explaining where their version of the shari'a comes from, just as it has made it unnecessary for them to adopt concrete policy proposals in other areas of ordinary politics.

In recent years, however, a new option has emerged. Experience has taught that where people vote freely, Islamists have a good chance of being chosen. This, coupled with the emergence of democracy as a universalist theory of government with few serious competitors, has led many Islamists to adopt the rhetoric and sometimes the practices of democracy.[18] A lively Islamist literature has sprung up around the question of the compatibility of Islam and democracy. In particular, the literature often poses the question of whether divine sovereignty may be reconciled with what is taken to be the democratic principle of popular sovereignty.

The arguments that surround this question are involved, and I have discussed them in detail elsewhere.[19] Here, it should be enough to note the conclusion adopted by most Islamists: mainstream Islamism has in principle accepted the compatibility of the shariʿa and democracy. The mechanisms of reconciliation differ from thinker to thinker, but the most prominent proposed solution is for the constitution of the Islamic state to acknowledge divine sovereignty rather than establish popular sovereignty and then use it to enact Islamic law. On this theoretical model, the people function somewhat as the ruler did in the classic constitutional order: they accept the responsibility for implementing what God has commanded.

In effect, the mainstream Sunni Islamist position is that the democratically elected legislature should draft and pass laws that incorporate the content of Islamic law. The constitution of the state will say that Islam or Islamic law is either "the source of law" or "a source of law.[20] Where Islamic law does not provide univocal answers, the democratically chosen Islamist legislature is supposed to use its discretion to adopt laws infused by Islamic values.

The result is a fundamental change in the theoretical structure underlying Islamic law: the shariʿa is *democratized* in that its keeping is given over to a popularly elected legislature charged with enacting legislation derived from the source that is the shariʿa. In practice, this democratization of the shariʿa means that the interpretation of what the shariʿa requires is in the first instance put in the hands of the public and its elected representatives. The problem of the missing scholars who traditionally interpreted the shariʿa is addressed through the substitution of the elected legislature for the scholars. Applied Islamic jurisprudence of the kind once practiced by the scholars remains only insofar as it might be relevant to a public that wants to draw upon Islamic legal reasoning to ascertain what Islamic law requires.

Yet for all its creativity as a solution to the challenges of modernity and egalitarianism, the democratized shariʿa faces a deep question: to what does it owe its authority? If the shariʿa is to be the ultimate source of law in the state, then it must also be the source of law for the constitution. Yet the constitution is enacted by actually existing citizens, and legislation is enacted by actually existing legislators. The classical shariʿa dealt with this problem by claiming that the task of the scholars was solely to interpret, not to legislate, and that this task of interpretation was authorized by the shariʿa itself. For the democratized shariʿa, the same answer cannot be given, because laws are actually being passed and because the classical shariʿa nowhere envisions an elected legislature.

For the democratized shariʿa, the answer is complex and uncertain. Laws that touch directly on the express content of the shariʿa are said to be merely confirmatory of its content and practical in its implementation. If the scholars disclaimed legislation, the legislature disclaims interpretation. Other laws are said to embody the spirit of the shariʿa or of Islam, the content of which anyone may (in theory) judge. These answers, though theoretically imprecise, are practically viable much of the time. They break down, however, when we consider the following conceptual difficulty: what if the legislature gets it wrong?

The Constitutionalization of the Shariʿa

To state the problem precisely: what must be done if the laws passed by the legislature, whether enacted in good faith or not, do not correspond to the "true" content of Islamic law or values? The problem threatens to make a mockery of the democratized shariʿa. The Prophet is reported to have said that "my people shall not agree upon an error"—the source of the legal doctrine of consensus as a source of law. But very early in Islamic history, the scholars interpreted this remark to mean that the community *of scholars* would never agree on an error. If the democratic public (through its elected representatives) may err, how can that public be said to control the shariʿa, which must be authoritative in order to be binding?

Here the Islamist constitutional theorists have proposed an answer that resonates in contemporary global constitutional practice.[21] They recommend judicial review of legislative action, not merely to ensure its compliance with the constitution, but to guarantee that it does not violate Islamic law or values. What is sometimes called a "repugnancy clause," mandating that a judicial body overturn laws that are repugnant to Islam, has made its way into several recent constitutions that seek to reconcile Islam and democracy. It may be found in the Afghan constitution of 2004 and the Iraqi constitution of 2005.[22]

The origins of what I shall call "Islamic judicial review" are disparate and merit our attention. Before we turn to these origins, however, it is important that we notice the functional effect of this model. Islamic judicial review transforms the highest judicial body of the state into a guarantor of conformity with Islamic law. Such a court is not a legislative entity in the first instance. But like any court empowered to exercise judicial review of legislation, it effectively has both the power and the responsibility to mandate certain legal outcomes by prohibiting others as violating the relevant judicial norm. Critics of judicial review everywhere complain that the act of review is in fact an act of legislation; and if truth be told, in an important sense, the role of suspending or overturning legislation is itself inherently legislative.[23]

The legislative character of judicial review is characteristically softened by the claim that all the court is doing is interpreting the relevant standard and applying it to the legislative act under review. In other words, a court engaged in Islamic judicial review must necessarily be engaged in the act of interpreting the content of Islamic law or Islamic values or whatever else the constitution says is the relevant standard to apply when legislation is evaluated. The interpretation adopted by the court will be binding insofar as the legislature will lack the power to countermand it and must adopt new legislation conforming to the dictates of the judicial body.

It emerges that Islamic judicial review puts the court in a position resembling that once occupied by the scholars. Like the scholars, the judges of the reviewing court present their actions as interpretations of Islamic law. Like the scholars, the judges issue decisions from which there is no possibility of appeal. And like the scholars, the judges of any court engaged in judicial review will find themselves involved in a very delicate balance of power between their own institution and the other sources of authority, such as the legislature and the executive branch.

But of course the judges engaged in Islamic judicial review are *not* the scholars. Islamist constitutions may adopt Islamic judicial review, but they usually leave in place the existing judiciary, manned not by scholars but by judges trained in the civil law tradition. The sources of the judges' institutional and personal legitimacy, therefore, will be very different from those of the classical scholars. Even if, as in Afghanistan, some might be trained primarily in the shari'a, their authoritative position would depend not upon the extent of their scholarly qualifications, but instead on the fact of their holding office. To paraphrase an adage associated with the U.S. Supreme Court, they would be infallible because they are final, not final because infallible. Not unlike the colonial judges whom they replaced, these judges, untrained in Islamic law, have the legal-constitutional obligation to ascertain the content of "Islamic law" or "Islamic values" and to apply it to real cases.[24]

The judges engaged in Islamic judicial review will also differ from the scholars in that their task is expressly assigned to them by a written constitution. Unlike the scholars, they get their jobs through a selection process subject to the full range of political maneuvering available in a modern state. Countries differ with respect to their method for selecting high court judges, with methods of appointment ranging from direct election all the way to self-selection by a committee of the judiciary. Everywhere that judicial review flourishes, judicial selection is understood to be political and is avidly contested by those who care about constitutional outcomes.

Perhaps most significant, judges engaged in Islamic judicial review would differ substantially from their scholarly predecessors in that they would have to share their legislative-interpretive authority with a democratically elected legislature. The constitutional obligation to adopt Islamically oriented legislation falls in the first instance to the legislative body. The constitutionalized shari'a will therefore sit alongside the democratized shari'a of which we have previously spoken. One could, of course, have a legislature bound to follow Islamic values without a check in the form of judicial review; but one cannot really imagine the latter without the former.

It can be predicted that an effective and consistent practice of judicial review will lead the legislature to frame its enactments in terms likely to be acceptable to the reviewing court. A democratically elected legislature responsible for enacting provisions in accordance with—or at least not repugnant to—the shari'a represents a unique step in the history of Islamic law: the democratization of the law so that the ordinary citizen might, through his elected representatives, shape the content of laws that govern him.

The Islamist Constitutional Model: Promising or Futile?

Depending upon one's perspective, the prospect of a democratized shari'a, supervised by the constitutionalized process of Islamic judicial review, will appear either as the most promising development in Islamic law since the collapse of Ottoman Empire, or else as a disaster waiting to happen. The optimistic point of view would begin by observing that the failures of the Tanzimat reforms—especially the retraction of the constitution and the abolition of the legislature by Abdulhamid II—ushered the governance of many majority-Muslim countries down the path of unbridled executive power. Transferring true lawmaking power from the scholars to an elected legislature, by contrast, might have led to much better results, and even to the mutation of the scholars' rule of law tradition into a modern and democratic form.

To the optimist, the democratized shari'a today represents nothing less than the opportunity to get back on track: to put the Islamic tradition of the rule of law back into contact with the democratic impulses that have recently emerged in the Muslim world. On this rather sanguine account, it has taken the Islamists with their nostalgic yearning for Islamic justice to get beyond the state-centered forms of governance associated with corrupt executivism. The Islamists, according to this way of thinking, are doing the Muslim world a huge favor by circumventing the scholars and seeking the restoration of the Islamic state in an altered and democratic form.

From the pessimist's perspective, however, the aspiration to restore the rule of law through the combination of an elected legislature, a powerful judiciary, and a secret recipe of Islamic values is the worst sort of naive fantasy of political-legal reformation. The ideas here are abundant; but the institutions are missing. A democratically elected legislature may be wished into existence—as the experiences of Iraq and to a lesser degree Afghanistan suggest—but that does not mean it will have either the incentives, the experience, or the confidence to become something greater than the sham legislatures that prevail in many places in the Arab and Muslim worlds.

The same is doubly true of a court supposed to exercise Islamic judicial review. It is one thing to appoint members of a judicial body and instruct them that they have the power to overrule the legislature and ignore the executive. It is quite another for anyone else in the system, in the other branches of government, in the general public, or in the police and administration, actually to obey the commands of the court. The temptation for the court to pull its punches and become ineffectual or else to overreach and attempt to assume quasi-dictatorial powers will be very great.

It takes generations for newly designed institutions to catch on and begin to perform their functions. Even then, the functions that they perform often turn out to be different from those envisioned by their designers. Political culture must be just so. Institutions must have or develop constituencies that can support them in the constitutional crises that must inevitably arise. The stars must be aligned perfectly so that qualified, intelligent, farsighted statesmen come to occupy key positions. The odds that all these conditions will converge are very small—so small as to be negligible.

Most devastating, the one institution that historically played a central role in establishing and maintaining the rule of law in Islamic states has been destroyed. According to this view, the Islamists' cardinal error was the abandonment of the scholars and the failure to recognize or acknowledge the scholars' central and irreducible role in the formation and functioning of the classical Islamic state. To restore Islamic law without restoring the scholars to their place is to ensure the failure of the project by cutting off the organism from the soul that inhabits it. As the living, breathing doctrine of an institutional force capable of generating and conferring legitimacy, the shari'a made the classical Islamic state into a success. As a set of rules on paper, even enacted by a democratic legislature and even enforced by a high court, the shari'a lacks the institutional framework to which it could otherwise give life. Without the shari'a, the scholars are nothing. But it may be that without the scholars, the shari'a, too, cannot live up to its aspiration to structure a just and balanced state.

The Iranian Option

Islamic judicial review as proposed by Sunni Islamists owes much to the spread of constitutional judicial review globally in the period since World War II. It may possibly be connected, albeit in inverted form, to British colonial provisions that permitted the operation of local customary or religious law—provided its provisions were not deemed repugnant to equity, natural justice, and the conscience of the Western judges who would apply them.[25] The term "repugnancy clause," often used to describe the provisions that appear in the Iraqi and Afghan constitutions of the middle of this decade, is borrowed from the Pakistani constitution, which in the wake of British colonialism prohibited any law "repugnant" to the "injunctions of Islam."[26] In the postcolonial period, it was plausible for courts and constitutions to turn this tool of Western supervision and potential disapproval of Islamic legal practice against itself, replacing the requirement of conformity to Western notions of justice with their own, distinctively Islamic judicial veto.

But the Islamic version of the practice, as deployed, for example, in the Iraqi and Afghan constitutions, has another important source. The first instance of Islamic judicial review appeared in the Iranian constitution of 1906–7, a document produced by and for Muslims, with the active participation of scholars and without substantial Western interference or influence. The story of the Shi'i scholars of Iran, their form of Islamic judicial review, their short-lived constitution, and their eventual return to power with the rise of Ayatollah Ruhollah Khomeini provides a fascinating and illuminating counterpoint to the story of scholarly decline and Islamist rise I have been telling in the Sunni context. It reveals a road not traveled in the Sunni world, and in the process, the rewards and the risks of a resurgent scholarly class.

The Iranian constitutional story, from its origins in the constitutional revolution of 1905–11 through the Islamic revolution of 1979 and beyond, must be seen in the light of the distinctive political and constitutional theory of Shi'ism. Like Shi'i legal theory more generally, Shi'i constitutional thought shares some basic features with its Sunni counterpart. But the distinctive theological position and historical development of Shi'ism ensures that the differences are salient and important.

The crucial founding difference between Shi'ism and Sunni Islam lies in a disagreement over a constitutional question, namely, the problem of succession to the Prophet. As we saw in Part I, the Sunni approach to succession, by requiring that the best-qualified candidate be chosen and endorsed by those with power to "bind and loose," created a decisive opportunity for the scholars, who quickly claimed that role for themselves as a matter of law, if not as a matter of actual fact. This claim, I argued, was symbolically important to the scholars' successful quest to establish themselves as arbiters of the legitimacy of the ruler and enforcers of his duty to follow the law as they interpreted it.

For the Shi'is, however, succession ran through the Prophet's bloodline, to his cousin and son-in-law 'Ali, and then to 'Ali's descendants, the martyred Husayn and his successors. From a strictly logical standpoint, this reliance on a quasi-divine imam as the successor to the Prophet (for Shi'ism enhanced the personal qualities of the imam to a point just short of deification) would have meant a comparatively reduced role for the scholars, since their ability to interpret the law would surely have been subordinated to the greater capacities of God's representative on earth. In the event, however, the opposite happened. Mainstream Shi'is came to believe that the line of succession ended with the twelfth imam in the line, the so-called hidden

128

imam whose occultation is expected to end some day with his messianic reemergence.

For Twelver Shi'ism, then—though not for Shi'i sects like Isma'ilism or Zaydism who revere a living imam as the shadow of God on earth—the basic state of human governance is to live *without* the guidance of the true and legitimate ruler, who remains absent. In the imam's absence, the Shi'i scholars argued, it fell to them to explicate the divine message and the law in which it is expressed.[27] This role, not altogether dissimilar to that of the Sunni scholars, left the Shi'i scholars in fact more powerful than their Sunni counterparts. Where Sunni scholars had to contend with a caliph who had his own extensive constitutional rights and responsibilities, Shi'i scholars were interacting with rulers who either fell far short of the combined religious-political power of the true imam, or else—if they were Sunni—were in principle completely illegitimate to the Shi'i way of thinking.

As it happened, for reasons having little to do with their theology, Shi'is were rarely in a position where they held political power. As a result, the constitutional theory of Shi'i governance was, in the medieval period, underdeveloped relative to Sunni constitutional theory. In the handful of medieval Shi'i states, such as Fatimid Egypt, the status of the scholars vis-à-vis the government was as a result strikingly similar to the relationship in the self-same place under Sunni government. This began to change when the Safavid dynasty of Iran embraced Twelver Shi'ism in the sixteenth century. After the Safavids' two hundred-plus years of rule, subsequent Iranian dynasties kept the Safavids' Shi'ism, so that for half a millennium Iran's rulers have professed the faith of the party of 'Ali. The role of the scholars has therefore had to be developed in the context of a comprehensive constitutional theory for the era of the hidden imam.

What emerged in Iranian Shiʻism—perhaps because of the traditional Persian genius for bureaucratic organization, derived from the pre-Islamic empire and never entirely forgotten—was a highly developed, formalized system of scholarly hierarchy. The Shiʻis developed a range of official ranks, beginning with the ordinary mullah and going all the way to ayatollah, "sign of God." Ranks and promotions within ranks came to be granted and administered by scholarly faculties gathered in the great Shiʻi centers of learning in Najaf and Kerbala, and, much later (in the twentieth century), Qom.[28]

The upper echelons of these ranks included the qualification of *mujtahid*—meaning one who is entitled to engage in independent interpretation of the law. This term was familiar to classical Sunni legal thought, where it was used as well to designate the highest level of scholarly attainment. Mawardi's idealized caliph was supposed to have attained this level of scholarship, though it is doubtful that any Sunni ruler ever did. Over the centuries, however, as the tradition of Sunni legal thought developed, it became increasingly rare for any scholar to assert that he was so qualified. The term developed a kind of frightening quality as scholars insisted that they were doing nothing more than applying the teachings of their predecessors. Indeed, so unusual did the claim to independent interpretive capacity become in the Sunni context that it was sometimes said that the gates of independent interpretation (*ijtihad*) were closed—an observation that was taken as an axiom by Western students of Islamic law until it was called into question in the 1980s.[29]

No such retreat from independent interpretation occurred among the Shiʻi scholars. To the contrary, they became increasingly confident in their ability to ascertain the content of the divine will on the basis not simply of legal materials, but of broader philosophical materials as well. The tradition of medieval Islamic philosophy, which drew on Plato, Aristotle, and much of the rest of the Greek philosophical corpus, lived on in Iranian Shi'i scholarship long after it had disappeared from the Sunni intellectual world. Always the preserve of an exclusive intellectual elite, this philosophical tradition persists to this day in Qom, where mullahs study medieval and contemporary philosophy alongside their shari'a curriculum.

Schooled in these texts, which may plausibly be read to emphasize the responsibility of the elite to make decisions for the multitude, the mullahs have remained confident in the ability of the scholarly class to guide the community. A fatwa issued on a political subject by a Shi'i scholar may contain the bare bones of an argument drawn from political theory—not the involved legal reasoning typically found in legal responsa issued by Sunni scholars. When, for example, Ayatollah 'Ali al-Sistani, the most influential Shi'i cleric in Iraq, issued his 2003 fatwa demanding that the Iraqi constitution be drafted by an elected body representative of the demographics of the Iraqi polity, the document was less than a page long. It made no reference to any source of authority other than the internal logic of democratic political theory.[30]

This background brings us to the leading role of the scholars in Iran's constitutional revolution of 1905–11.[31] The political context for these events was the decline of Iranian imperial power, which had been chipped away by Russia and Britain during the Great Game of the nineteenth century. Iran managed to avoid the humiliating fate of colonization suffered by so many other Muslim countries during this era, but the old regime was weakened to the point of collapse. By 1905, the state found itself in serious fiscal trouble, having borrowed from the West and spent the money quickly on the basic necessities of state maintenance.

Internal weakness is always the great facilitator of constitutional reform. Iran's merchant middle classes, frustrated at the burdens of taxation generated by the government's fragile financial situation, looked to the scholars with whom they had become allied in earlier struggles against government changes to the existing economic order.[32] Sensing their power relative to the state, the scholars rose to the occasion, lending their support to a popular movement that demanded a reform package and respect for Islamic legal norms. The scholars—or at least an important group of them—found themselves part of a reform movement that embraced an innovation for Iran: a written constitution.

The notion of written constitutionalism was naturally a tricky one from the scholars' standpoint. More sophisticated both theoretically and politically than Sunni scholars of the same era, the Shi'i scholars of Iran recognized that the very fact of a written document tended to undercut their own authority over law and legal institutions. At the same time, they seem to have believed that a written constitution would also afford the public some advantage in limiting the power of the new rulers who were waiting in the wings. A lively scholarly debate ensued: would a written constitution necessarily violate the shari'a? Could the two be reconciled through a constitution guided by shari'a principles? Or was the impossibility of implementing the shari'a fully in the absence of the hidden imam a reason to accept limited government as the best of a bad situation?[33]

The written constitution that was drafted (in two stages) offered an answer.[34] Though based roughly on the Belgian constitution, it nevertheless treated the shari'a as an independent source of legal and constitutional authority. The Shi'i scholars backed the document once it had been supplemented by Islamizing elements that entered in the second stage of the drafting process.[35] Crucial to the structure of this "shari'a constitution" was a provision creating a body composed of senior

132

scholars with the authority to review legislation and ascertain whether it conformed to the dictates of the shariʻa.[36] The structure of this provision provided the groundwork for Islamic judicial review as adopted a century later in the Afghan and Iraqi constitutions; and it also inspired the Council of Guardians in Khomeini's Islamic revolutionary constitution.

There is little historical work on the specific intellectual origins of this important constitutional clause, perhaps because its influence turned out to be indirect and long-term rather than immediate.[37] Its design may have been consciously influenced by Platonic political theory as was the case for its notorious descendant, the Council of Guardians; or it may simply have been a pragmatic attempt to formalize scholarly power in written terms. It is unlikely to have been influenced by Western notions of judicial review, since these were largely absent from most Western constitutional arrangements at the time, including the Belgian model primarily followed. At the turn of the twentieth century, judicial review was a prominent constitutional feature only in the United States, which had not yet begun to exert the kind of influence over global constitutional norms that would come with its ascendancy to world power status.[38] Whatever its exact antecedents, it would seem that Iran's version of judicial review was homegrown: the product of the scholars' attempt to craft for themselves a formal supervisory role in accordance with the structure of written constitutionalism.

Viewed in hindsight through the lens of the Islamic revolution, to which we shall shortly turn, the Islamic judicial review clause may be seen as an early and incomplete attempt to put the scholars at the top of the legal-constitutional hierarchy. Yet in political rather than intellectual terms, the Iranian constitutional revolution was a failure. Various rulers of the late Qajar dynasty sought to rescind or ignore it until 1925, when power passed into the hands of the Pahlavi dynasty who ruled the country until the last shah fled in 1979. The constitution itself was never enforced seriously, and Islamic judicial review never played a meaningful constitutional role.

Rule by Scholar

The role of the Shi'i scholars in the constitutional revolution of 1905–11, especially their success at adding Islamic judicial review to the constitutional text, suggests that those scholars were more sophisticated than their Sunni contemporaries. Coupled with their prominence today in the present Iranian regime, it might lead one to expect that they would have retained a central place in Iranian political life through the century. Yet this was not uniformly true. Although it is fair to say that as a class, the Shi'i scholars never declined to the extent that their Sunni counterparts did,[39] nevertheless under Pahlavi rule, beginning in 1925, the scholars' power declined precipitously.

The reason was that the Pahlavis decided to secularize Iranian society almost to the extreme extent pursued by Kemal Pasha in Turkey. As in Turkey, traditional forms of dress were banned, including the headscarf or veil for women and traditional men's headgear. Also as in Turkey, the government attempted to bring Islamic institutions under state control. Here the Pahlavis were less successful than Ataturk. Seminaries remained places where quiet opposition to the secularization policies could be voiced. Nevertheless, over the years, the most prominent clerical critics of the regime found it necessary to go into exile. Khomeini himself was exiled in 1963 after calling for the overthrow of the government.[40] He spent years in the seminaries of Iraq before being forced to Paris, whence he came to displace Shah Reza Pahlavi in 1979.

The secularization of Iranian society met with success only among the educated classes, however—maybe because of the persistent strength of the scholars compared to their collapse in Turkey. When the shah's weakness became manifest, secular intellectuals including communists joined forces with the scholars in making the revolution of 1979. Their reasoning was that the scholars would have greater credibility with the poor and dispossessed than did urban, educated elites. Khomeini had indeed made the downtrodden the subject of his special concern.[41]

The secular revolutionaries seem to have expected that once the revolution occurred, they would be able to dispense with the mullahs. They could not have been more wrong. Khomeini's effective dispatching of communists and other secular allies presaged the way Islamism would survive and indeed flourish in the late twentieth century even as communism died out.[42] It was this postrevolutionary purge, rather than the demographic composition of the first revolutionaries, that made the 1979 revolution "Islamic." It took a parallel purge of moderate, nonscholarly Islamists like President Abo'l-Hasan Bani-Sadr for Khomeini and his followers to make the revolution specifically clerical.[43] With these nonscholars out of the way, Khomeini was free to establish a constitutional structure that would correspond to his own version of Shi'i political theory.

Khomeini's constitution gave institutional form to his novel version of *velayat-e faqih*, the authority of the scholar-jurist. The nineteenth-century predecessor of this view consisted in essence of the notion that, in the absence of the imam, the scholars were assigned the authority to oversee government. Khomeini took this idea and made it at the same time truly radical: in his account, the scholars would directly exercise the power to rule. When the shah fled, Khomeini presented himself as the scholar most qualified to govern in his stead. As a popular slogan of the revolutionary moment had it, "the Shah has gone, the Imam has come."[44]

The idea that the scholars as a class would rule directly was without precedent in Islamic history. That one scholar in particular would lead them was in some ways more remarkable still. The rule of the supreme leader who must be a scholar was perhaps easier to imagine in a Shi'i context, since the leader was almost a kind of undeclared returned imam (as indeed some of Khomeini's followers called him) who combined political and religious authority. He was also, in Platonic terms, a philosopher-king, one whose personal judgment would be better than subordination to a set of written laws.[45]

Completing the Platonic structure of supreme leader was the Council of Guardians, a body composed of scholars who would review all legislation for its Islamic content. Eventually, the council would come to play the key role in vetting candidates for office and even selecting a new supreme leader after Khomeini's death. With power vested in the supreme leader and the council, the directly elected president would become a figure of sharply limited power, able to do just what the leader and council allowed, and no more—as the reformist president Mohammad Khatami would later learn to his chagrin. The elected legislature would be composed of representatives precleared for their friendliness to the scholars and to their version of Islamic governance.

The extraordinary character of this whole arrangement was that it turned the historical role of the scholars neatly on its head. Where the scholars had traditionally functioned as a balance against the executive authority of the ruler, now the scholars for the first time actually were the ruling class. The scholars' stranglehold on the composition of the legislature ensured that no other base of power existed to counterbalance the scholars. The result was an unfettered, supreme scholarly executive.

From the standpoint of constitutional design, the consequences of this model come as no surprise. An executive who is not counterbalanced will tend toward abuse of power and absolutism. Just as in other majority-Muslim countries the disappearance of the scholars as a balancing force facilitated unchecked executive power, so, too, in Iran, the ascension of the scholars to the executive seat brought about constitutionally disfiguring executive power. Government in Iran under the mullahs has been as lacking in basic freedoms, in transparency, and in the due process of law as government in most other Muslim states that are not run by the scholars—sometimes even more so.

The Iranian example shows that the revival of the scholarly class, if such a thing were possible in the Sunni world, would not on its own solve the problem of autocracy. What is important to creating just, functioning constitutional government under the rule of law is not the presence or absence of the scholars, but *balance*—which the scholars traditionally provided. Iran also shows that there is nothing inherent about the scholars' education in the law that makes them uniquely able to govern justly when not counterbalanced by alternative forces. The shari'a has the capacity to function as a tool for the fair administration of justice. But like any other legal system, it cannot do so if it is not embedded in a constitutional order in which the dictates of the law are enforced by institutions with the incentive to act justly and the real-world powers to see that their rulings are executed in practice. The shari'a is no magic solution to the problem of the rule of law.

The brief life of the Taliban regime in Afghanistan also makes it clear that it is not the Shi'i character of the Iranian regime that has led to its internal corruption. The Taliban, indirectly emulating the Iranian model (despite Iran's nonsupport of their regime), set out to create the world's first Sunni state governed by scholars. Mullah Omar, the Taliban leader, turned out to be no better than any other leader ruling without substantial counterbalance. Of course the Taliban were mostly not fully qualified scholars, but, as their name implied, madrasa students whose training left them well short of membership in the scholarly class. Their rulings—like the walling-in of suspected homosexuals—often hewed more closely to Pashtun custom than to any tenet of the shari'a. But it would not have made a decisive difference to the overall quality of their governance had they been fully trained as scholars.

The Shari'a as a Last Resort

Although the examples of Iran and Taliban Afghanistan show the limits of government by scholars, there is another context in which the local administration of justice by scholars in charge of shari'a courts has proven slightly more promising. In failed states, quasi-Hobbesian environments where literally no group of persons and institutions can claim to exercise a monopoly on the use of legitimate force, local inhabitants have shown a willingness to turn to self-established shari'a courts to engage in the most basic form of dispute resolution. Such courts typically make no claim—and have no capacity—to do much more than determine basic private-law questions of mine and thine, and encourage local strongmen to enforce their rulings. They have no formal coercive power at their disposal; they rely for their jurisdiction on the consent of private parties who are prepared to treat the judgment of the court as binding. They are therefore very far from the position of authorities who are not counterbalanced by other institutional forces. Rather, it might be said that the forces of disorder limit such courts' authority—the same forces of disorder that drive litigants into their arms.

The most prominent recent example of shari'a courts operating in what is otherwise a governmental vacuum is that of Somalia, where more than a decade of failed governments led to a situation in which no organized authority exercised sovereignty over the tribal leaders who filled the daily role of authority. Tribal customs can, of course, include legal practices and institutions, and do in some places elsewhere in Africa. It seems, however, that no such legal mechanisms were operating within Somali tribes, a result perhaps of the general breakdown of Somali society. More important, tribal justice is never very effective at resolving disputes between members of different tribes, who naturally expect not to get a fair hearing in the courts of rivals. As a result, with no state in place and no plausibly effective tribal alternative, some Somalis were prepared to look to institutionally isolated scholars to resolve disputes according to what were understood as neutral Islamic legal principles.

The result was the creation of a series of local Islamic courts, which seem to have arisen independently but gradually came into loose relation with one another to form a network. In a process reminiscent of the hypothetical genealogy of government authority given by Robert Nozick in *Anarchy, State, and Utopia*,[46] these affiliated courts began to make modest governmental claims. In particular, they began to demand an end to the arbitrary violence that characterized Somali social relations. Having begun by providing law, they moved on to attempting to provide order—the most basic function of any protogovernment.

The shari'a-courts movement had been making broader governmental claims for only a few months when the United States reacted. In 2007, claiming to perceive in the movement a potential willingness to harbor terrorism, it supported Ethiopia in a coordinated military campaign to defeat the poorly organized protogovernment and replace it with a different government that was being returned from exile through force. The shari'a-courts movement scattered in the face of the Ethiopian invasion, but the new government proved itself unable to exercise actual governing authority, and the situation on the ground began quickly to resemble the anarchic state that had existed before the courts movement began. The courts movement had to regroup and begin again in areas outside the government's reach—which is to say, much of the country.

But the intervention that short-circuited the shari'a-courts movement should not distract us from the most important lessons of its brief rise. Perhaps any self-constituted court would have been better than nothing for ordinary Somalis, regardless of the legal system it purported to apply. Nevertheless the Islamic courts had a set of special advantages for the task of combating disorder. First, because most Somalis are Muslim, they would probably have expected that the substantive rulings of the courts would be basically fair and just. Second, the scholars—few and poorly trained though they might be—still possessed enough residual respect and authority as interpreters of the law that they were able to constitute these courts under the most difficult conditions imaginable, and at considerable personal risk. This authority must have helped protect them from threats by tribal leaders on whose power they necessarily encroached. Third, Islam possesses a universalist capacity to offer a point of loyalty transcending particularistic tribalism. This feature was essential to the Prophet Muhammad's initial project of uniting disparate tribes under a single banner, and even though Islam never eliminated tribalism or its identities, it has, at least in cities, historically been very successful at replacing tribal dispute resolution with Islamic legal institutions. Indeed, this might be described as the task to which Islamic law is most suited. Somalia, then, was a case of back to the future for Islamic courts.

The Future of the Islamic State

The failures and distortions of Islamic states governed directly by scholars have not dulled the appetite of ordinary voters in many majority-Muslim countries for Islamic governance of some sort. The most striking, consistent, and hard-to-explain electoral phenomenon in the Muslim world in the latter part of the twenty-first century's first decade is the continuing popularity of Islamic parties. This trend began with the Algerian elections of 1990, and it has not yet reversed course.

In Arab states, where free elections are difficult to come by, Islamist political parties have been successful wherever they have been allowed to participate. In Iraq, not only did the Shi'i Islamists win a plurality that enabled them to form a government, but even in Sunni areas it was Islamist parties who did the best. In Lebanon, another Arab country with relatively free elections, Shi'i Hezbollah has consistently done better than anyone would have expected. The Palestinian election of 2006, another example of a relatively free vote, featured Islamist Hamas winning enough seats to form a government of its own, albeit one that proved unable to cohabit with the presidency of Fatah leader Mahmoud Abbas. Meanwhile, carefully controlled elections that have taken place in Egypt, Morocco, Jordan, Bahrain, Kuwait, and even on a tiny scale in Saudi Arabia have all demonstrated that Islamist political parties can win most of the seats they are permitted to contest.

141

Almost two decades after the Algerian elections that revealed the democratic appeal of the Islamists, it is far too late to assert that these results reflect mere protest voting. No doubt voters are fed up with autocratic and ineffective regimes that happen to be secular. The terrible track record of Fatah, for example, surely contributed to the success of Hamas. But at the same time, the Islamists are no longer a flash in the pan without a clear governing platform. They have become regular participants in both elections and government, not to mention masters of a political discourse that can be seen on satellite television throughout the region. The voting public in the Arab world understands who the Islamists are and essentially what their platform is.

Nor can the success of Islamists be explained solely by poverty or the efforts of their organizations in delivering social services. Again, Islamists have often been helped by the perception that they care about the poorest citizens and are prepared to do something for them. In Palestine, in Egypt, and elsewhere, Islamist politics were jump-started by grassroots organizing that grew from social projects. But Islamist voters come from the middle class, not just the poorer classes. By now, voters also understand that they can glean the benefit of Islamist social services without being governed by Islamist political parties.

It is time, therefore, for observers outside the Arab world to accept what most of those inside already have: Islamist politics have become a reality in Arab electoral space. Elections are only one way for an organization to gain power, of course. Alongside social services and grassroots activism, there is also violence of the kind wielded by hybrid militia-political parties like Hezbollah and Hamas. Islamists have shown they are willing to use all of these tools. The fact remains, however, that mainstream Islamists are also fully prepared to use nonviolent electoral means even where free elections continue to be unavailable. It is today impossible to imagine Jordanian politics without the Islamic Action Front, a political party associated with the Muslim Brotherhood.[47] We cannot presently understand Moroccan politics without grasping the twin roles of the polite, government-sanctioned Islamist Justice and Development Party and the shadowy, outlawed, yet increasingly important movement known as Justice and Improvement.

Beyond the Arab world, Islamist electoral politics has flourished in other Muslim-majority countries. The most prominent example is Turkey, where the moderate Islamist AK Party (whose full name, again, includes the word "justice") led by Recep Tayyip Erdogan has been remarkably successful over the last several years in moving forward the national agenda of accession to the European Union with its requirements of economic liberalization and respect for human rights. The secularist military keeps a watchful eye out to discourage over-Islamization, and the direct implementation of the shari'a is therefore not an agenda item for the AKP. But there can be no mistaking the party's religious orientation, nor does anyone forget that Erdogan himself was banned from politics for his Islamist tendencies before leading his party to power and becoming one of the most successful democratic Turkish politicians in a century.

The positive story of Turkey may be tempered by the case of Pakistan, where Islamism has a more antidemocratic cast despite the participation of Islamist parties in elections, with increasing effect in each successive campaign. But in Pakistan as in Turkey, Islamism has certainly become a permanent force, or as close to permanent as any movement may be considered in the shifting vicissitudes of Pakistani politics. And unlike Turkey, in Pakistan the constitution accepts and even encourages a substantial role for Islam. The Pakistani constitution—what-

143

ever its other limitations, as applied—retains its formal recognition of the role of Islamic law; and Pakistan is officially an "Islamic Republic." The high court has adjudicated blasphemy cases and continues to address questions of Islamic law in various ways. If a wholly Islamic state is still a fantasy of the most extreme Islamists, Pakistan's formal constitutional structure already embodies many of the goals of mainstream Islamists.

Where is all this Islamism going? Given the steadily increasing success of Islamist political parties, will we see more Islamic states—Islamic to one degree or another? Will there be more systems embodying some form of shari'a governance, whether democratized or constitutionalized or both?

One possibility is that we will see a slight modulation of autocratic governments in the direction of greater public emphasis on Islam, without underlying substantive change. Certainly that would be the preference of the autocrats, and probably of the United States, which fears giving even moderate Islamists the opportunity to take power in elections. Cautious recognition of Islamic symbolism is the tried-and-true path of Muslim kings and dictators, and it would be naive to say definitively that they will not be able to sustain it over time.

Yet governments in the Muslim world are under increasing pressure from inside and outside to give voice to popular political movements within their countries. Those movements are, at this historical juncture, predominantly Islamist. The most probable scenario is that Islamists' calls for the shari'a in its democratized or constitutionalized form will increasingly be heeded. Islamist political forces will participate in the formation of governments and will find themselves able, within certain political limitations, to adopt aspects of their programs and try them out in practice.

In some cases, as in Iraq, Afghanistan, and Palestine, constitutional change will be followed by violence, disorder, and ineffective government, so that Islamist ideas do not get a chance to be fully implemented. Certainly the willingness of many Islamist parties to maintain violent military wings decreases the likelihood of Islamist institutions that actually function. As a result, the capacity of Islamist government to build and develop institutions has not really been tried. Iraq could have been the greatest test case, but its descent into disorder, facilitated by the inadequacies of the U.S. occupation, has destroyed its exemplary status.

Where Islamists win elections in a functioning state, the United States and other regional actors are sufficiently nervous about Islamist government that opponents—including those prepared to use force—will typically find external support for undermining the Islamists in power. This paradigm was set first in Algeria, where France and the United States supported the military regime in canceling the election results and squelching Islamist rule. We have seen it again in Palestine, where the United States encouraged Fatah to deny Hamas the role in government that was in theory supposed to come with its electoral victory, ultimately providing a motive for the Gaza takeover that split the Palestinian Authority in two. As of this writing, there is still no case where an Islamist government has come to power by peaceful means and been allowed to govern peacefully.

But so far, we also do not have examples of Islamist governments taking power under basically peaceful conditions and *failing* to govern. Until Islamists actually do have the opportunity to govern and so to succeed or fail, the public can be expected to continue voting for them. It is not that Islamists are less susceptible than other political movements to the test of effective government. It is, rather, that the appeal of the Islamists' platform relies so heavily upon the ideals of functioning government and a just legal system that the public will not be satisfied until they have had a chance to see whether the Islamists can actually carry it off. If contemporary governments in the Arab or Muslim world managed to deliver basic political justice for their citizens, no doubt the appeal of the Islamists would be reduced. Yet there is little prospect of such political justice in the foreseeable future so long as unchecked executive power continues to be the dominant constitutional mode in those countries. So long as all-powerful executives continue to rule unjustly—which is to say, so long as they continue to rule—there will be a hunger for an alternative.

CONCLUSION

Islamism, Institutions, and the Rule of Law

ALL THIS BRINGS us to the question of whether, in power, Islamists could in fact bring about the rule of law. As the case of Iran shows, a government organized in the name of Islam can be as constitutionally corrupt as a secular autocracy and so may find itself equally unpopular with its citizens. If the Islamists cannot deliver political justice, they will find themselves discredited like their predecessors. Yet if the Islamists can deliver on their promise of justice, it seems more than possible that a return to some form of shari'a governance could spread throughout the Arab and Muslim worlds.

Whether this will happen depends ultimately upon the Islamists' ability to develop new institutions that would find their own original and distinctive way of giving real life to the ideals of Islamic law. This could be an Islamically oriented legislature, infused with the spirit of a democratized shari'a; or it could be a court exercising Islamic judicial review to shape and influence laws passed in its shadow. In either case, however, such an institution on its own would not be enough to deliver the rule of law. Under the influence of the legislative branch, the judicial branch, or even both, the executive branch would have to develop a commitment to obeying legal and constitutional judgments.

147

How that happens—how an executive accustomed to over-weening power comes to be subordinated to the rule of law—is one of the great mysteries of constitutional development worldwide. In some cases, total revolution is necessary. A new, weak executive may have little choice but to obey the law if it wants to establish its own constitutional legitimacy. It is tempting to imagine that such revolution might be necessary to eliminate the overly powerful executives who dominate Arab and Muslim states. But total revolution has an extremely bad track record in recent decades, at least in majority-Muslim states. The revolution that replaced the shah in Iran ended up just as top-heavy from a constitutional standpoint. And the equally revolutionary dreams of Ahmed Chalabi and Paul Wolfowitz for Iraq have so far proven fruitless, as Saddam's Ba'thist autocracy has been replaced by an anarchic situation that so far has not provided the stability necessary for effective new institutions to emerge.

Gradualist constitutional change therefore looks more attractive than ever. This in turn makes Islamism seem appealing, because of its willingness to adapt already existing political institutions by infusing them with Islamic values and some modicum of Islamic law. Perhaps it is even possible to imagine Islamist electoral success putting pressure on executives to satisfy the Islamist demand for political justice embodied in the call for adoption of the shari'a. This would then also require a transformation of judicial culture, akin to the one that has occurred recently in Pakistan, in which judges would come to think of themselves as agents of the law rather than as servants of the state.

We have seen that the shari'a, considered both as an actual set of historical practices and as a contemporary ideology, can provide the necessary resources for such a rethinking of the judicial role. In its essence, the shari'a aspires to be Law that applies equally to every human, great or small, ruler or ruled. No one is above it, and everyone at all times is bound by it. Though the constitutional structure that historically developed to implement the shari'a afforded the flexibility necessary for practical innovation and effective government, that structure also maintained the ideal of legality. Judges who are devoted to the shari'a in this sense are therefore devoted to the rule of law, and not the rule of the state. The legitimacy of a state in which officials adhere to this structure of beliefs would depend upon the state's faithfulness to implementing the law.

But as we have also seen, the ideals of the rule of law are not and cannot be implemented in a vacuum. For that a state needs actually effective human institutions, reinforced by regular practice and the recognition of the actors within the system that they have more to gain by remaining faithful to its dictates than by deviating from them. The classical Islamic constitutional order had such institutions; but it lost them when it fell. What must rise again in their place cannot be the same as what came before. The new Islamic state, if it is to succeed, can learn from aspects of traditional practice, but it must do for itself the difficult and slow work of establishing new institutions with their own ways of operating that will gradually achieve legitimacy.

There are lessons here for those outside and inside majority-Muslim states who hope to see meaningful constitutional-legal reform that will move governments away from autocracy without casting them into anarchy. Our best efforts must be devoted to building institutions that perceive themselves and are perceived by the public as committed to the rule of law. Aid can be made contingent on respect for the roles of courts and legislatures. Executives can be pressured to adhere to the laws and judgments of coordinate branches of government—even (or especially) when no direct foreign interest is at stake. Exemplary institution-builders can be recognized with carefully placed praise calculated to enhance rather than detract from their domestic legitimacy.

In this undertaking, a healthy skepticism for mere symbols is a necessary tool. "Training" of judges and other legal elites by outside experts, even when it is sensitive to the particularities of local conditions, can strengthen legal and judicial institutions; but it takes much more overt political and financial support when their legitimacy is challenged by the executive. Conferences and declarations on judicial independence have their place[1] but it takes sustained engagement to change the mind-set of judges, not to mention their real-world institutional power.

When new legal and constitutional institutions, Islamic or otherwise, do manage to enter onto the scene and make their play for legitimacy, it is imperative to support them. If the United States acquiesces in the executive's efforts to repress them, it sends the message that the United States does not care about the rule of law. By contrast, the Islamists continue to promise justice and the rule of law via the shariʿa. It may be tempting to block the Islamists by denying them institutional power. But this strategy is likely to backfire, since the public will see it for what it is, and it will reconfirm the view that the Islamist aspiration to justice is opposed by the West and the local autocrats.

The Islamists' odds of success at the ambitious endeavor of creating and renewing institutions to deliver the rule of law may never be high. The reinvention of democracy in the modern era was an improbable—and partial—accomplishment, one that required its practitioners to meld old ideas with new practices, often without acknowledging the difference. One reason why so many states today are eager to adopt wholesale the constitutional architecture of other places is the very great difficulty of creating such a system from scratch. Borrowing, with all of its limitations, still seems easier than invention. Nevertheless, with all its risks and dangers, the aspiration to re-create a system of government that draws upon the best of the old while coming to terms with the new is as bold and noble a goal as can be imagined.

ACKNOWLEDGMENTS

THIS BOOK grew from almost a decade's reflection—practical and theoretical—on constitutional change in the Islamic world. Although the ideas in it began to crystallize in the surreal setting of the former Republican Palace in Baghdad, they could not have been reduced to writing without support from the Carnegie Corporation, the Council on Foreign Relations, the New York University School of Law, and the Harvard Law School. I refined many of the arguments here in a seminar I conducted at the Yale Law School, and would like to thank the student participants in that group, as well as the Yale Middle East Legal Studies Seminar and the Harvard Law School faculty workshop, where I presented partial drafts. I received particularly helpful criticism from Abdulaziz Al Fahad, a true gentleman-scholar; steady guidance from Heather Schroder of ICM; and patient engagement from Fred Appel of Princeton University Press. I also benefited from the research assistance of Navid Sato, Kalina Denkova, Ian Mitch, Shalev Roisman, and Ben Owen, as well as the comments of Jill Goldenziel, Anver Emon, Yasir Kazi, and Andrew March.

153

NOTES

NOTE ON PROPER NAMES: After the first use, I have dropped the definite article "al" from before Arabic proper names. I hope the added clarity for the newcomer will compensate for any discomfiture felt by the initiate.

Introduction

1. See Gallup World Poll, Islam and Democracy, available at http://media .gallup.com/MuslimWestFacts/PDF/GALLUPMUSLIMSTUDIESIslamand Democracy030607rev.pdf. In Egypt 66 percent and in Pakistan 60 percent say shari'a must be the only source of legislation. In Jordan the number is 54 percent. For further consistent polling data, see "Revisiting the Arab Street from Within," Center for Strategic Studies, Amman, Jordan (February 2005), 52–55 available at http://www.jcss.org/SubDefault.aspx?PageId=37&PollId= 140&PollType=3.

For a more detailed breakdown of attitudes regarding application of the shari'a in government, see Nancy J. Davis and Robert V. Robinson, "The Egalitarian Face of Islamic Orthodoxy: Support for Islamic Law and Economic Justice in Seven Muslim-Majority Nations," in *Values and Perceptions of the Islamic and Middle Eastern Publics*, ed. Mansoor Moaddel (New York: Palgrave Macmillan, 2007), 126–59.

2. Throughout this book, when I refer to Islamists or Islamism, I have in mind mainstream Sunni Muslim activists loosely aligned with the ideology of the transnational Muslim Brotherhood (MB). Under the slogan, "Islam is the solution," the Brotherhood broadly embraces electoral politics, but without eschewing the use of violence in some circumstances, notably against those whom it defines as invaders in Iraq and Palestine. Radical Islamists are those who reject any participation in democratic politics; liberal Islamists accept many of the goals of establishing Islamic law but advocate more liberal

155

interpretations of the shari'a than do mainstream Islamists. In support of various claims about the mainstream Islamist movement, I shall cite documents available on the Web sites of the Muslim Brotherhood and its global affiliates. These sites change frequently, and I have given the titles of the documents as they appear and have provided up-to-date URLs when possible. Where these passages from the Web sites appear in English, the text is presented verbatim, without corrections for grammar or diction. Where the text appears in Arabic, that is indicated and a translation is provided. See, for example, the document entitled "The Principles of the Muslim Brotherhood": "The introduction of the Islamic Shari'a as the basis controlling the affairs of state and society" is presented as the first key pillar to the MB's call. "The Principles of the Muslim Brotherhood," *IkhwanWeb.com*, June 8, 2006, http://www.ikhwanweb.com/Article.asp?ID=813&LevelID=2&SectionID=116. In "Muslim Brotherhood Initiatives for Reform in Egypt," political reform is also pointed out as a "starting point to reform the rest of all life walks which witness a speedy decline almost hitting the bottom line in Egypt and Arab, as well as Islamic worlds," *IkhwanWeb.com*, June 10, 2007, http://ikhwanweb .com/Article.asp?ID=797&SectionID=-1&Searching=1. In regard to the shari'a, the same document presents the Brotherhood's "mission" to work on "the establishment of Allah's Shari'a as we believe it to be the real effective way out of all sufferings and problems, both on the internal front and the external one—be these political, economic, social or cultural. This mission could be achieved through building the Muslim individual, Muslim family, Muslim government and the Muslim state that leads Islamic countries, gather all Muslims, regain Islamic glory, gives lost Muslim land back to its owners and carry the flag of the call to Allah, thus making the world happy via the teachings and right of Islam. This is our target and this our method, as Muslim Brotherhood." See also "The Electoral Programme of the Muslim Brotherhood for Shura Council in 2007," http://www.ikhwanweb.com/Article .asp?ID=822&LevelID=1&SectionID=116. See also the (Jordanian) Islamic Action Front Program for 2003 Parliament Elections, http://www.jabha.net/ body7.asp?field=jbh%20&id=2.

3. The concept of democracy is discussed in "Muslim Brotherhood and Democracy in Egypt," *IkhwanWeb.com*, June 13, 2007, http://www.ikhwan web.com/Article.asp?ID=808&SectionID=-1&Searching=1. See also the statement of Dr. Mohamed Habib, deputy chairman of the Muslim Brotherhood, "Democracy is Our Choice Toward a Civil State," *IkhwanWeb.com*, June 13, 2007, http://www.ikhwanweb.com/Article.asp?ID=807&SectionID

=-1&Searching=1. In addition, in "The Principles of the Muslim Brotherhood," fifteen principles are introduced as a "compendium for the democratic principles" for which the MB stands, *IkhwanWeb.com*, June 8, 2006, http://www.ikhwanweb.com/Article.asp?ID=813&LevelID=2&SectionID=116. Another example is Islamic Constitutional Movement, "Who Are We," entitled "Towards Dedication to Democracy in the Country," available in Arabic at www.icmkw.org.

4. Cf. Nathan Brown, *The Rule of Law in the Arab World: Courts in Egypt and the Gulf* (Cambridge: Cambridge University Press, 1997), 11 ("In many ways, the popularity of calls for the application of the Islamic *shari'a* flows directly from the continuing appeal of this image of law [i.e., the rule of law].")

5. Terminology is the special preserve of academic dispute; and within its expanses may be found the still more restricted—and more intensely disputed—precincts of periodization, where roam the historians. These cannot be entirely avoided in a book about constitutional change and development, but it is not my intention to make any new contribution to either. When I speak of the traditional or the classical Islamic constitution, I mean to describe a constitution that changed and evolved enormously over many centuries while still maintaining some sense of continuity. When exactly it took a recognizable form is itself a question difficult to answer; certainly the Abbasid caliphs would have recognized it clearly, and it seems likely that the Umayyads would have as well. Before that it is rather difficult to say; for a creative and fascinating treatment of the early period, see Patricia Crone and Martin Hinds, *God's Caliph: Religious Authority in the First Centuries of Islam* (Cambridge: Cambridge University Press, 1986); see also Patricia Crone, *God's Rule: Government and Islam* (New York: Columba University Press, 2004), 3–47. I could have called it the medieval Islamic constitution, but the term is misleading insofar as the Ottoman empire up until 1924 retained some recognizable though distinct version of it, and the Saudi state today operates on the basis of what is also in a meaningful sense a version. The term "classical" might be misleading to a professional student of Islam, since the term is sometimes used to refer to a distinct period of Islamic history, running roughly from 692 to 945. See, e.g., Marshall G. S. Hodgson, *The Venture of Islam* (Chicago: University of Chicago Press, 1974), 1:231–496. Although I use the term much more broadly, it captures something important when it is used to distinguish the Islamic constitution of the premodern era from the new Islamic constitutions of the modern, Islamist era. I was sometimes

tempted to speak of the ancient Islamic constitution, by analogy to the English idea of the "ancient constitution"—cf. J.G.A. Pocock, *The Ancient Constitution and the Feudal Law: A Study of English Historical Thought in the Seventeenth Century* (Cambridge: Cambridge University Press, 1987)—but the term "ancient" as used here is itself technical to English constitutional history. To get some sense of the enormous difficulty of adopting any periodization or terminology in the Islamic context, see the chart in Hodgson, *The Venture of Islam*, 1:234.

6. A working definition of the Islamic constitution may be found in Crone, *God's Rule*, 28: "a set of rules that allocated functions, powers, and duties among the various agencies and offices of government and defined the relationship between them and the public." On the classical Islamic constitution and the place of law in it, see Sherman A. Jackson, *Islamic Law and the State: The Constitutional Jurisprudence of Shihab al-Din al-Qarafi* (Leiden: E. J. Brill, 1996). This work remains one of the only recent texts addressing the interrelationship between classical Islamic law and the classical Islamic constitutional order. For Jackson's review of the most important older Orientalist work on Islamic constitutional thought, including important works by Gibb, Coulson, Watt, Lambton, and Rosenthal, see xxxv–xl. See also Hodgson, *The Venture of Islam*, 1:315–58 for what he calls the "shar'i Islamic vision," which is recognizably a constitutional picture.

7. The term for a scholar of the law is *faqih* (pl. *fuqaha'*). In this book I use the term "scholars" to refer more broadly to the social class from which the *fuqaha'* came. When I refer to legal scholars more narrowly, I use the term "jurists."

8. Compare Richard Bulliet, *The Case for Islamo-Christian Civilization* (New York: Columbia University Press, 2004), 64. Bulliet describes the shari'a as a constraint on rulers and the scholars as the vehicles of that constraint; see 65–66. More significant, Bulliet proposes that what he calls "anticlerical" government efforts facilitated the rise of autocracy: "*Theory predicted that rulers freed from the bonds of the sharia would seek absolute power, and they regularly lived up to that expectation*" (73, emphasis in original). He also mentions Ottoman codification in this context; see 74–75. In his seminal discussion, Bulliet does not, however, provide an account of why the collapse of the scholars' influence should have mattered if the law's constraint was historically only theoretical. And he repeats the familiar idea that "sadly, as every historian of Islam knows, in practice the ulama seldom succeeded in preventing despotism." My own approach in this book is to argue for a robust classical constitutional structure that in fact was largely efficacious, with well-

known exceptions. The eventual failure not simply of the scholars but of the entire constitutional regime of which they formed a crucial part can, I shall propose, explain much of the dominating executive power that followed.

9. Douglass North, *Institutions, Institutional Change and Economic Performance* (Cambridge: Cambridge University Press, 1990). Or consider this eclectic definition: "Institutions are the durable fabric which structures relations between classes and agents. They provide the social nexus of communication which provides shared symbols, sites of practice, and some degree of certainty which reduces the social cost of human intercourse." P. O'Hara, *Marx, Veblen and Contemporary Institutional Political Economy* (Cheltenham: Edward Elgar, 2000), 37.

10. This is not to deny the complex ongoing role of the scholars in contemporary Muslim societies, studied most prominently by Muhammad Qasim Zaman, *The Ulama in Contemporary Islam: Custodians of Change* (Princeton: Princeton University Press, 2002), especially 144–91. Rather, my argument is that the scholars' role no longer suffices to counterbalance executive power as it once did.

11. See Chibli Mallat, *The Renewal of Islamic Law* (Cambridge: Cambridge University Press, 1993).

12. Egypt and Pakistan each have provisions making Islamic law into a source of law. Egypt does not have a repugnancy clause barring legislation that violates the shari'a.

13. Cf. Jackson, *Islamic Law and the State*, xiv–xv.

14. Noah Feldman, *After Jihad: America and the Struggle for Islamic Democracy* (New York: Farrar, Straus & Giroux, 2003).

Part I: What Went Right?

1. Myself not excluded. See Feldman, *After Jihad*, 20, though my central claim there is that political Islam has succeeded because of its emphasis on justice; see 50.

2. See, for example, "Hamas Legislative Elections Program": "The Islamic Law will be the source of Palestinian legislation, the three branches, legislative, executive and judicial are to be separated," http://www.ikhwanweb.com/lib/Hamas_Program.doc. See also "The Electoral Programme of the Muslim Brotherhood for Shura Council in 2007," http://www.ikhwanweb.com/Article.asp?ID=822&LevelID=1&SectionID=116, and the strategic goals of

the Islamic Constitutional Movement listed in the statement entitled "Who Are We" (in Arabic), http://icmkw.org/about_us.aspx.

3. Nevertheless it remains the official slogan of the Muslim Brotherhood, despite detailed debates within the movement over its precise meaning. The introductory part of the "Electoral Programme for Shura Council in 2007" discusses the reasons for adopting the slogan and provides answers to the question why Islam is the solution.

4. See, e.g., Montesquieu, *Lettres Persans*, in Montesquieu, *Oeuvres completes*, ed. Courtney et al., vol. 1 (Oxford: Voltaire Foundation, 2004).

5. See Weber on *kadijustiz* (qadi justice) in Max Weber, *Economy and Society: An Outline of Interpretive Sociology*, ed. Guenther Roth and Claus Wittich, trans. Ephraim Fischoff et al. (Berkeley and Los Angeles: University of California Press, 1978), 3:976; Bryan Turner, *Weber and Islam* (London: Routledge & Kegan Paul, 1978), 109–21. For a valuable discussion, see Baber Johansen, *Contingency in a Sacred Law: Legal and Ethical Norms in the Muslim Fiqh* (Leiden: Brill, 1990), 47–51 and especially n. 183, where he points out that the term was coined not by Weber but by Richard Schmidt. Felix Frankfurter brought Weber's image into the American legal canon. *Terminiello v. City of Chicago*, 337 U.S. 1, 11 (1949) (Frankfurter, J. dissenting) ("We do not sit like a kadi under a tree, dispensing justice according to considerations of individual expediency").

6. See David S. Powers, *Law, Society, and Culture in the Maghrib, 1300–1500* (Cambridge: Cambridge University Press, 2002), 23–52; and see the introductory essay by the editors in *Dispensing Justice in Islam: Qadis and Their Judgments*, ed. Muhammad Khalid Masud, Rudolph Peters, and David Powers (Leiden: Brill, 2006), 1–44. See also Bulliet, *The Case*, 65–66 (noting that scholars "have thoroughly and repeatedly refuted [Weber's] stereotype"). This does not mean, of course, that in the Islamic world historically and today there are not officials who resolve disputes through fact gathering and adjudication without constant or detailed reference to legal materials. On the twentieth-century examples of these, see the anthropological work of Lawrence Rosen, especially *Anthropology of Justice: Law as Culture in Islamic Society* (Cambridge: Cambridge University Press, 1989). But the existence of such courts does not undercut the principle of the rule of law or the overall structure of Islamic legality, any more than small-claims courts in the United States or even state-authorized arbitral bodies—with their similar informality and casual attitude toward procedure—negate the rule of law there. Complex legal systems frequently comprise numerous component parts employing vastly different methods for the dispensation of justice. Rosen's critique of much

academic work on Islamic law as too focused on theory rather than practice is an important one, but it must not be extended to the point of misleadingly characterizing the constitutional structures of Islamic law in neo-Weberian terms on the basis of one subset of legal institutions.

7. There were sometimes unqualified judges in outlying areas, and perhaps their judgment would have looked like Weber's "qadi justice." But when the Islamic legal community found out about them, it tried to replace them with judges who knew the law. See, for example, Bernard Haykel, *Revival and Reform in Islam* (Cambridge: Cambridge University Press, 2003), 127 (giving the example of Shawkani urging the removal and replacement of unqualified judges).

8. On the muftis, see the collection *Islamic Legal Interpretation: Muftis and Their Fatwas*, ed. Muhammad Khalid Masud, Brinkley Messick, and David S. Powers (Cambridge: Harvard University Press, 1996), particularly 3–32.

9. A valuable bibliography of the "extensive" literature on the scholars is presented in Zaman, *The Ulama in Contemporary Islam*, 193 n. 3.

10. Crone and Hinds, *God's Caliph*. See also Crone, *God's Rule*.

11. A recent work, Knut Vikør, *Between God and the Sultan: A History of Islamic Law* (Oxford: Oxford University Press, 2005), admirably incorporates the wealth of scholarship in Islamic law in the last several decades into its presentation and should now probably supplant the classic N. J. Coulson, *A History of Islamic Law* (Edinburgh: Edinburgh University Press, 1964), as a general historical introduction.

12. Wael B. Hallaq, *The Origins and Evolution of Islamic Law* (Cambridge: Cambridge University Press, 2005), 63–101, offers the best recent overview. See also Wael B. Hallaq, *A History of Islamic Legal Theories: An Introduction to Sunni Usul al-Fiqh* (Cambridge: Cambridge University Press, 1997), 1–35.

13. Edward Coke, *Reports* 3:vi–vii. For a discussion, including John Selden's skepticism, see J. W. Tubbs, *The Common Law Mind: Medieval and Early Modern Conceptions* (Baltimore: Johns Hopkins University Press, 2000), 141–54.

14. On the dispute regarding Fadak, near Medina, see *Encyclopaedia of Islam*, 2nd ed., q.v. "Fadak."

15. The question of the accuracy of these reports as a general matter has been a charged one in Islamic legal studies. The most skeptical view was that of Joseph Schacht, *An Introduction to Islamic Law* (Oxford: Oxford University Press, 1964). Some more recent works of scholarship tend to credit much more material. The point I wish to make is simply that the problem of distin-

guishing accurate from inaccurate was already an important one to early Muslim scholars.

16. For the hadith, see, e.g., *Sunan Abi Dawud*, bk. 25:3634.

17. On the schools as institutions, see George Makdisi, *The Rise of the Colleges: Institutions of Learning in Islam and the West* (Edinburgh: Edinburgh University Press, 1981); Jackson, *Islamic Law and the State*, 69–73; 103–23; Vikør, *Between God and the Sultan*, 89–113.

18. The classic source for this formulation is Schacht, *Introduction to Islamic Law*, 5 ("it was created and developed by private specialists; legal science and not the state plays the part of a legislator, and scholarly handbooks have the force of law").

19. Michael Cook, *Commanding Right and Forbidding Wrong in Islamic Thought* (Cambridge: Cambridge University Press, 2000).

20. See, e.g., Montgomery Watt, *Islamic Political Thought: The Basic Concepts* (Edinburgh: Edinburgh University Press, 1968), 73. To be fair to Watt, he also acknowledged that the rulers could not modify the law, suggesting that through the use of administrative regulations the law could be circumvented by the ruler (75). See also Turner, *Weber and Islam*, 115–16.

21. A representative comment is Bulliet's assertion that "as every historian of Islam knows, in practice the ulama seldom succeeded in preventing despotism." *The Case*, 64. Another scholar writes as follows: "The fact that the case [that she is discussing] reflects a state of affairs between ruler and scholars that can be described as ideal (the ruler seeks and accepts the role of the scholars as advisers, counselors, and interpreters of the religious law) raises doubts about the historicity of the report." Maribel Fierro, "Caliphal Legitimacy and Expiation in al-Andalus," in Masud, Messick, and Powers, *Islamic Legal Interpretation: Muftis and their Fatwas*, 61. The fault is not with Fierro, who actually argues that the ruler in question, 'Abd al-Rahman II, did respect and solicit the scholars' opinions and treat them as "heirs of the Prophet."

22. Crone, *God's Rule*, 281–83. Crone then goes on to say that "[o]ne could not call this constitutional government even if virtue did occasionally win out" (284). A related argument is that "while the law prescribed limitations both on the authority of the ruler and the duty of obedience of the subject, it established no apparatus and laid down no device for preventing or challenging a violation of the law by the ruler, other than force." Bernard Lewis, *The Political Language of Islam* (Chicago: University of Chicago Press, 1988), 113.

23. Crone, *God's Rule*, 230, paraphrasing al-Baqillani.

24. See Henri Laoust, *Essai sur les doctrines sociales et politiques d'Ibn Taimiya* (Cairo: IFAO, 1939); E.I.J. Rosenthal, *Political Thought in Medieval Islam* (Cambridge: Cambridge University Press, 1958), 51–61; Ann K. S. Lambton, *State and Government in Medieval Islam* (Oxford: Oxford University Press, 1981), 138–51; and, more recently and controversially, Natana J. DeLong-Bas, *Wahhabi Islam: From Revival and Reform to Global Jihad* (Oxford: Oxford University Press, 2004), 250–56.

25. Qur'an 4:59. For Ibn Taymiya's views, see his *al-Siyasa al-shar'iyya fi islah al-ra'i wal-ra'iyya* (Cairo: Dar al-Sha'b, 1971) and many subsequent editions; in English, *Ibn Taimiyya on Public and Private Law*, trans. Omar A. Farrukh (Beirut: Khayyats, 1966). See also Kemal A. Faruki, *The Evolution of Islamic Constitutional Law and Practice from 610 to 1926* (Karachi: National Publishing House, 1971), 62–66.

26. Consider, for example, the rebellion against al-Hakam I in 805 in which Andalusian scholars were involved.

27. See, e.g., H.A.R. Gibb, "Al-Mawardi's Theory of the Caliphate," in his *Studies in the Civilization of Islam*, ed. Stanford J. Shaw and William R. Polk (Boston: Beacon Press, 1962), 161.

28. Abu al-Hasan al-Mawardi, *Al-Ahkam al-Sultaniyya wa-l-wilayat al-diniyya, The Ordinances of Government*. trans. Wafaa H. Wahba (Reading: Garret Publishing, 1996). On the question of priority, see Donald P. Little, "A New Look at al-Ahkam al-Sultaniyya," *The Muslim World* 64, no. 1 (January 1974): 1–15.

29. Ibid., 20.

30. Ibid., 36–37.

31. Ibid., 36.

32. Gibb, "Al-Mawardi's Theory of the Caliphate," says that Mawardi "implicitly excludes such an arrangement at the center" (163). But this is very much a matter of interpretation, based on Gibb's reading of Mawardi's treatment of the problem of the curtailment of the caliph's liberty (see 159–60), and Mawardi may well have meant his model to be applicable even to the caliphate itself.

33. See Lambton, *State and Government in Medieval Islam*, 107–29; Crone, *God's Rule*, 237–47; Leonard Binder, "Al-Ghazali's Theory of Islamic Government," *The Muslim World* 14, no. 3 (July 1955): 229.

34. Gibb, "Al-Mawardi's Theory of the Caliphate," 164.

35. Compare the notion of the circle of justice imported into medieval Islamic thought and regularly repeated in the mirrors-for-princes literature

advising kings on how to run their states. And see, e.g., Bulliet, *The Case*, 62 ("With justice and moderation the people will produce more, tax revenues will increase, and the state will grow rich and powerful").

36. Ibn Khaldun, *The Muqaddimah: An Introduction to History*, trans. Franz Rosenthal (New York: Pantheon books, 1958), 2:106.

37. Ibid., 106–7.

38. Ibid., 1:458–61.

39. For a useful overview covering nonshari'a courts and the question of jurisdiction, see Vikør, *Between God and the Sultan*, 189–205. On the Ottoman *kanun* version of these administrative regulations, see Colin Imber, *The Ottoman Empire, 1300–1650: The Structure of Power* (New York: Palgrave Macmillan, 2002), 244–51. The category of *ta'zir*, "an undefined penalty for an undefined delict," was acknowledged as the permissible province of the ruler and in this sense was "included into the shari'a"; the notion of *siyasa* extended to permissible state actions not covered by the law, which we might call executive prerogative. Johansen, *Contingency in a Sacred Law*, 216.

40. For a particularly sophisticated take, see Johansen, *Contingency in a Sacred Law*, 42–72.

41. See, e.g., Dominique Urvoy, *Le Monde des ulémas andalous du V/XIe au VII/XIIIe siècle: étude sociologique* (Geneva: Droz, 1978).

42. Ibn Khaldun, *The Muqaddimah*, 2:107.

43. On the *waqf* generally, see Vikør, *Between God and the Sultan*, 339–44; see also Richard van Leeuwen, *Waqfs and Urban Structures: The Case of Ottoman Damascus* (Leiden: Brill, 1999).

44. Of course even a canonical tax like the Fifth, or *khums*, was susceptible of interpretation. One account attributes the beginning of the Ottoman janissary cadre to the innovative legal suggestion that one-fifth of the slaves taken in war should be given to the state treasury. See Cemal Kafadar, *Between Two Worlds: The Construction of the Ottoman State* (Berkeley and Los Angeles: University of California Press, 1995), 112.

45. Cf. Powers, *Law, Society, and Culture in the Maghrib*, 82. ("Under any circumstances, the stoning of a member of the Muslim community would have been exceptional.") Powers is speaking of the Maghrib 1300–1500, but the point may be extended.

46. Cf. *Crowell v. Benson*, 285 U.S. 22 (1932).

47. See Richard Repp, "Some Observations on the Development of the Ottoman Learned Hierarchy," in *Scholars, Saints, and Sufis: Muslim Religious*

Institutions in the Middle East since 1500, ed. Nikki Keddie (Berkeley and Los Angeles: University of California Press, 1972), 17.

48. Colin Imber, *Ebu's-su'ud: The Islamic Legal Tradition* (Stanford: Stanford University Press, 1997). On the bureaucratization of the post, see Imber, *The Ottoman Empire*, 241–42.

49. Repp calls it a *cursus honorum*. Repp, "Ottoman Learned Hierarchy," 20. The first known formalization of the rules appeared in the second half of the fifteenth century (19 and n. 5). Eventually this system was corrupted through the ability of the sons of senior scholars to obtain advancement without demonstrating scholarly accomplishment (31)—an outcome all but impossible under the old reputation-based system.

50. See Imber, *The Ottoman Empire*, 126. Imber gives the first Ottoman use of the term as 1424 but says it was at the time "rhetorical rather than specific."

51. *Princeps legibus solutus est. Dig.* 1.3.31.

Part II: Decline and Fall

1. On the Western role in political change, see Roderic H. Davison, *Essays in Ottoman and Turkish History, 1774–1923: The Impact of the West* (Austin: University of Texas Press, 1990), 73–95.

2. The literature on the Tanzimat is voluminous. For a clear introduction, see Erik J. Zürcher, *Turkey: A Modern History* (London: I. B. Tauris, 1994), 52–74.

3. Like the strengthening of the bureaucracy, these reforms may have contributed to the process of weakening the scholars. Thus Nikki Keddie proposes that the scholars' power "declined in those states, like Egypt and the Ottoman empire, where the central government was able to strengthen itself significantly through the creation of a modernized army and central bureaucracy." Nikki Keddie, "The Roots of the Ulama's Power in Modern Iran," in Keddie, *Scholars, Saints, and Sufis*, 213. Chambers similarly argues that the replacement of the old Janissary corps with a modern army in 1826 robbed the Ottoman scholars of a traditional ally. See Richard L. Chambers, "The Ottoman Ulema and the Tanzimat," in Keddie, *Scholars, Saints, and Sufis*, 35. Yet it must be noted that Avigdor Levy shows that the scholars across the board supported the abolition of the Janissaries in the years before their revolt. See Levy, "The Ottoman Ulema and the Military Reforms of Sultan

Mahmud II," in *The Ulama in Modern History: Studies in Memory of Prof. Uriel Heyd*, ed. Gabriel Baer (Jerusalem: Israel Oriental Society, Asia and African Studies, No. 7, 1971), 21–23.

4. On the Ottoman *kanun*, the name for what I am calling administrative regulations, see Imber, *The Ottoman Empire*, 244–51.

5. For example, the Ottoman penal code of 1840, updated and supplemented in 1858, and the land code of the same year. Chambers, "The Ottoman Ulema," 44.

6. Chambers, "The Ottoman Ulema," 44–45.

7. See Uriel Heyd, "The Ottoman 'Ulema and Westernization in the time of Selim III and Mahmud II," in *Studies in Islamic History and Civilization*, ed. Uriel Heyd (Jerusalem, 1961), 96. ("The leading 'ulema . . . were not far-sighted enough to realize that the Westernizing reforms supported by them would eventually destroy the Islamic character of the Ottoman state.") The question is: why not? Heyd took the view that the upper echelon of the scholarly class was especially state-centered.

8. On Ahmed Cevdet Pasha, see Chambers, "The Ottoman Ulema," 43–44, and Richard L. Chambers, "The Education of a Nineteenth Century Ottoman Alim, Ahmed Cevdet Paşa," *International Journal of Middle East Studies* 4, no. 4 (October) 1973): 440–64. As Chambers recounts, Cevdet was compelled in 1866 to move formally from the scholarly class to the ordinary bureaucracy—as a result of rumors that he aspired to become grand mufti.

9. On this, see Hallaq, *A History of Islamic Legal Theories*, 210.

10. Vikør, *Between God and the Sultan*, 231.

11. Ibid. On codification and the "etatization of law" in the Ottoman reforms, see Sami Zubaida, *Law and Power in the Islamic World* (London: I. B. Tauris, 2003), 121–53.

12. The administrative apparatus of the scholars was independent, "subject only to the Sultan's prerogative to dismiss its chief"; and control of waqf revenues "made it, likewise, economically independent." Chambers, "The Ottoman Ulema," 35.

13. By contrast, China has long employed army officers without legal training as judges in rural areas, a trend that has only recently come under challenge. It might be fruitful to explore the similarities between the decline of the 'ulama and the decline of the Confucian class of scholar-administrator-judges in late imperial China.

14. For a good overview, see Nathan Brown, *Constitutions in a Nonconstitutional World: Arab Basic Laws and the Prospects for Accountable Government* (Albany: SUNY Press, 2002), 20–26.

15. Ottoman Constitution, Art. 87 (1876).

16. The Tunisian *qanun al-dawla* or "law of the state" of 1861 preceded it but did not use the same terminology. See Brown, *Constitutions*, 16–20.

17. Art. 4.

18. Art. 11.

19. Art. 5.

20. Brown reports comparisons both to the Belgian and Prussian constitutions; ibid., 21.

21. See Jeremy Bentham, *A Fragment on Government* (Cambridge: Cambridge University Press, 1988).

22. See Brown, *Constitutions*, 23.

23. Zürcher, *Turkey*, 83.

24. See Clark B. Lombardi, *State Law as Islamic Law in Modern Egypt: The Incorporation of the Shariʿa into Egyptian Constitutional Law* (Leiden: E. J. Brill, 2006), 60–100.

25. Farhat Ziadeh, *Lawyers, the Rule of Law and Liberalism in Modern Egypt* (Stanford: Hoover Institution, 1968), especially 78–82. On the period, see Afaf Lutfi al-Sayyid-Marso, *Egypt's Liberal Experiment: 1922–1936* (Berkeley and Los Angeles: University of California Press, 1977).

26. Zaman, *The Ulama in Contemporary Islam*, 21–37.

27. On the Iraqi constitution, see Brown, *Constitutions*, 42–46.

28. See Chibli Mallat, "Shiʿism and Sunism in Iraq: Revisiting the Codes," in *Islamic Family Law*, ed. Chibli Mallat and Jane Connors (London: Kluwer Law International, 1996). For the later vicissitudes of this code, see Noah Feldman, *What We Owe Iraq: War and the Ethics of Nation Building* (Princeton: Princeton University Press, 2004), 109–11.

29. On Sanhuri, see Enid Hill, "Al-Sanhuri and Islamic Law: The Place and Significance of Islamic Law in the Life and Work of ʿAbd al-Razzaq al-Sanhuri, Egyptian Jurist and Scholar 1895–1971," *Arab Law Quarterly* 3, no. 1 (February 1988): 33–64.

30. See Amr Shalakany, "Between Identity and Redistribution: Sanhuri, Genealogy and the Will to Islamise," *Islamic Law and Society* 8 (2001): 201; and see Shalakany's unpublished J.S.D. dissertation, "The Analytics of the Social in Private Law Theory: A Comparative Study" (Harvard, 2000).

31. See Zaman, *The Ulama in Contemporary Islam*, 21–31.

32. Clark Lombardi characterizes Sanhuri's method as "neo-taqlid," thereby emphasizing the distance of the legal sources from the legal problems to which they would be applied in the codes. Lombardi, *State Law as Islamic Law in Modern Egypt*, 92–99.

33. Contrast this interpretation with Watt's suggestion that concern for career advancement so "warped" the outlook of the scholars that "they chose subjects which were of no practical importance but in which they could demonstrate their mastery of scholarly techniques." Watt, *Islamic Political Thought*, 76.

34. Noah Feldman, "Religion and Political Authority as Brothers," in *Islamic Constitutionalism* (forthcoming).

35. Hasan Kayali, *Arabs and Young Turks: Ottomanism, Arabism, and Islamism in the Ottoman Empire, 1908–1918* (Berkeley and Los Angeles: University of California Press, 1997).

36. Egypt is often said to have an independent judiciary. For an important argument to this effect, see Brown, *The Rule of Law in the Arab World*. Yet despite some undoubted flashes of independent activity, the Egyptian judiciary does not, at present, represent a substantial counterbalance to the constitutional power of the president. By Brown's own account, the judiciary functions neither to establish the liberal legality associated with the phrase "rule of law" nor to legitimate the exercise of power by the executive. Instead it has fulfilled a "political" function, "augment[ing] the authority of the central state even as it placed (sometimes feeble) limitations on specific individuals and office holders" (128).

37. See, e.g., Ibn Taymiya, *Siyasa shar'iyya* (Ibn Taymiya on Public and Private Law in Islam), 188.

38. Madawi al-Rasheed, *A History of Saudi Arabia* (Cambridge: Cambridge University Press, 2002). On the earliest states, see 14–37.

39. On the Saudi legal and constitutional structure, see Frank Vogel, *Islamic Law and Legal System: Studies of Saudi Arabia* (Leiden: Brill, 2000).

40. Abdulaziz H. Al-Fahad, "Ornamental Constitutionalism: The Saudi Basic Law of Governance," *Yale Journal of International Law* 30 (2005): 375.

41. For the text of the fatwa and a sophisticated, historically grounded analysis, see Abdulaziz H. Al-Fahad, "From Exclusivism to Accommodation: Doctrinal and Legal Evolution of Wahhabism," *NYU Law Review*. 79, no. 485 (2004): 515–19. For bin Laden's reaction, see the translation in *Messages to the World: The Statements of Osama bin Laden*, ed. Bruce Lawrence (New York: Verso, 2005), 4–14.

42. See John S. Habib, *Ibn Sa'ud's Warriors of Islam: The Ikhwan of Najd and Their Role in the Creation of the Sa'udi Kingdom, 1910–1930* (Leiden: E. J. Brill, 1978), 122–23. The scholars declined to rule in the absence of prece-

dent; but Ibn Saʿud in an abundance of caution nonetheless banned "the use of the radio and telegraph in certain parts of the Kingdom" (123).

43. On the women drivers' movement and the reaction, see Al-Rasheed, *A History of Saudi Arabia*, 166–68. Cf. Al-Fahad, "Ornamental Constitutionalism," 383.

44. Rachel Bronson, *Thicker Than Oil: America's Uneasy Partnership with Saudi Arabia* (Oxford: Oxford University Press, 2006).

45. On oil wealth and democratization, a substantial literature has emerged discussing the so-called resource curse. See, for example, Michael Ross, "Does Oil Hinder Democracy?" *World Politics*, no. 53 (2001): 325–61.

46. The one case in modern history of revolution within an oil monarchy is that of Iran, which I shall discuss later. For our purposes now, it will be sufficient to note that the Iranian revolution of 1979 featured both of these elements, and that the memory of the fall of the shah is never very far from the minds of the Saudi royal family. Unlike Iran, Saudi Arabia lacks a large and self-confident middle class that might become fed up with the monarchy's consuming too much of the nation's wealth; and the Saudi government has done much to ensure that the poorest Saudis never feel the desperation that must have been felt by the Iranian lower class that flocked to support Ayatollah Ruhollah Khomeini. Also unlike Iran under the shah, the Saudi government has done all it can to keep the religious scholars close to it.

Part III: The Rise of the New Islamic State

1. A point already noted in the five volumes of the *Fundamentalism Project*, ed. Martin E. Marty and R. Scott Appleby (Chicago: University of Chicago Press, 1991–95).

2. Thus the draft of the Egyptian MB Party Platform affirms the equality of all citizens before the law and rejects any discrimination based on religion, race, or ethnic origin; Islamic Constitutional Movement, "Who Are We"—equality of citizens before law is stated as one of their strategic goals (in Arabic), http://icmkw.org/about_us.aspx. There is no incompatibility between egalitarianism and reliance on an ideological vanguard, as may be attested by the examples of communism and feminism.

3. On the early intellectual history of the Muslim Brotherhood, particularly its complex attitude toward the scholars, see Ibrahim M. Abu-Rabiʿ,

169

Intellectual Origins of Islamic Resurgence in the Modern Arab World (Albany: SUNY Press, 1996), 62–91; and see the description of the scope of the activities of the Brotherhood in "Who Are We."

4. Islamists were exposed to Protestant ideas indirectly, filtered through the lens of Western modernism—itself a product of the fusion of Reformation ideology and Renaissance classicism. Another possible source is the Protestant missionary–founded educational institutions like the American Universities of Beirut and Cairo, which played important roles in the birth of Arab nationalism. See Heather Sharkey, *American Evangelicals in Egypt: Missionary Encounters in an Age of Empire* (Princeton: Princeton University Press, 2008).

5. See, e.g., "The Electoral Programme of the Muslim Brotherhood for Shura Council in 2007." The MB also discusses its "mission" to apply the shari'a in "The Muslim Brotherhood's Program [for 2005 Parliamentary Elections]." This can also be seen in the text of "Hamas Legislative Elections Program"; making Islamic law the basic source of legislation holds the first place in the Legislative Policy and Judicial Reform section.

6. See John Esposito and Dalia Mogahed, "Battle for Muslims' Hearts and Minds: The Road Not Yet Taken," available at http://www.muslimwestfacts .com/content/26866/Battle-Muslims-Hearts-Minds-Road-Yet-Taken.aspx (reporting Gallup poll results in forthcoming work by the same authors).

7. On the delicate relationship between Islamists and scholars, whom the Islamists wish to sideline but not disrespect, see Abu-Rabi', "Intellectual Origins"; and see also Aziz Ahmad, "Activism of the Ulama in Pakistan," in Keddie, *Scholars, Saints, and Sufis*, 261–62 (describing the views of the influential Islamist Abu'l A'la Mawdudi). Notice that the scholars, in the Islamist vision, end up resembling Protestant ministers, teachers of personal piety without special authority.

8. For example, "The Principles of the Moroccan Party of Justice and Development" (the official party Web sites are currently unavailable). Also, the MB's view of the Islamic state is presented in "The Electoral Programme of the Muslim Brotherhood for Shura Council in 2007."

9. See "Reading into the Muslim Brotherhood Documents," under the heading "Pillars of a Regime":

> [T]he Muslim Brotherhood considers that Islam presents general rule principles which can deal with the problems that the society faces, like unemployment, inflation, housing, price hikes, collapse of manners and drugs and other problems. The most prominent of these principles are:

1. Preparing and forming a Muslim individual who observes Muslim conscience and morals to be an effective element in building facilities.

2. Reforming the country in media, educational, economic, social and political perspectives.

3. Depending on Islamic reference as a basis.

IkhwanWeb.com, September 29, 2006, http://ikhwanweb.com/Article.asp?ID= 818&LevelID=2&SectionID=116. See also "Muslim Brotherhood and Democracy in Egypt":

> Hasan al-Banna set a rule for the Muslim Brotherhood about how to deal with any new idea. He described the Muslim Brotherhood saying, "The most precise word to describe the movement is 'Islamic'. This word carries an extensive meaning, aside from the narrow one that is perceived by most people, since we believe that Islam is an integrated meaning that regulates all matters of life and sets an accurate rule for every issue. It is not helpless concerning the problems that face people, and the necessary systems that may lead to reforming them." (*IkhwanWeb.com*)

10. Islamic Constitutional Movement, list of strategic goals in "Who Are We"; "Hamas Legislative Elections Program."

11. See the discussion of Ibn Taymiya's views, above.

12. For example, the Moroccan Party of Justice and Development, "Why Justice and Development? Justice Providing Equal Opportunities and Development Beyond the Material Concept." Also, the party provides a description of the concept of justice in the Party Principles (currently unavailable from its official English Web site); in addition, al-Adl wal-Ihsan provide a definition of "justice" in "Who Is al-Adl wal-Ihsan?" http://www.aljamaa.net/ar/detail_khabar.asp?id=6364&IdRub=27 [in Arabic].

13. Sayyid Qutb, *Social Justice in Islam*, trans. John B. Hardie (American Council of Learned Societies, 1953; reprint, Oneonta, NY: Islamic Publications International, 2000).

14. *Ma'alim fi l-tariq.*

15. See the statement of Dr. Morsi, MB Executive Bureau Member, "Dr. Morsi: MB Has a Peaceful Agenda," *IkhwanWeb.com*, http://ikhwanweb.com/Article.asp?ID=1024&LevelID=1&SectionID=70.

16. The platform of the Muslim Brotherhood in Egypt, for example, calls for legal reform and indeed for the "rule of law," associated with Islamic governance. See "MB Brotherhood Initiatives for Reform in Egypt," *Ikwhan Web.com*, on general principles in the field of legal reform.

17. On '*adala*, see *Encyclopaedia of Islam*, 2nd ed., q.v. 'Adl.

18. The Islamic Constitutional Movement presents its "Dedication to Democracy in the Country" in "Who Are We." The establishment of justice takes first place in the scale of their priorities; second, they put freedoms in light of the shari'a rules. See also the statement of Dr. M. Habib, Deputy Chairman of the Muslim Brotherhood, "Habib: Democracy is Our Choice Toward a Civil State," *IkhwanWeb.com*, June 13, 2007, http://ikhwanweb.com/Article.asp?ID=807&SectionID=-1&Searching=1.

19. See Feldman, *After Jihad*; also Noah Feldman, "Shari'a and Islamic Democracy in the Age of al-Jazeera," in *Shari'a: Islamic Law in the Contemporary Context*, ed. Abbas Amanat and Frank Griffel (Stanford: Stanford University Press, 2007), 104–119.

20. For example, the text of "Hamas Legislative Elections Program"—Islamic law is stated to be "the basic source of legislation"; see also chapter 3 of "The Electoral Programme of the Muslim Brotherhood for Shura Council in 2007," in which the MB state their determination to "amend laws and make them accordant to the Islamic Shari'a as being the main source of legislation." *IkhwanWeb.com*, June 14, 2007, http://ikhwanweb.com/Article.asp?ID=822&SectionID=-1&Searching=1.

21. See Feldman, "Shari'a and Islamic Democracy."

22. A form of Islamic judicial review is possible even without a repugnancy clause. In Egypt, for example, the provision making Islamic law the source of law has produced a body of constitutional case law. See Lombardi, *State Law as Islamic Law in Modern Egypt*.

23. See, for example, Ran Hirschl, *Toward Juristocracy: The Origins and Consequences of the New Constitutionalism* (Cambridge: Harvard University Press, 2004).

24. Cf. Lombardi, *State Law as Islamic Law in Modern Egypt*, 2–3 (considering different views of the nature of the interpretive undertaking of secular constitutional courts applying some version of a shari'a provision).

25. See H. H. Marshall, *Natural Justice* (London: Sweet and Maxwell, 1959), 165–73.

26. The provision was retained in the Constitution of 1973. See article 227 (1). On its origins, see Charles H. Kennedy, "Repugnancy to Islam—Who Decides? Islam and Legal Reform in Pakistan," *International Comparative Law Quarterly* 41 (October 1992): 769, 770–71.

27. On Shi'i constitutional thought, see, with caution, Abdulaziz Sachedina, *The Just Ruler in Shi'ite Islam: The Comprehensive Theory of the Jurist in Imamite Jurisprudence* (Oxford: Oxford University Press, 1988); and the devastating but illuminating review by Hossein Modaressi, "The Just Ruler

or the Guardian Jurist: An Attempt to Link Two Different Shi'ite Concepts," *Journal of the American Oriental Society* 111, no. 3 (1991): 549–62. Cf. Nikki Keddie's assertion that the scholars' claim to interpret the will of the imam is a late one "with no basis in early Twelver theory." Keddie, "The Ulama's Power in Modern Iran," 217.

28. Keddie notes the significance of the location of the major centers of learning, outside Safavid control, and therefore outside the sphere of political influence of centralizing governments in the nineteenth century. Keddie, "The Ulama's Power in Modern Iran," 226.

29. Wael B. Hallaq, "Was the Gate of Ijtihad Closed?" *International Journal of Middle East Studies* 16, no. 1 (March 1984): 3–41.

30. See Feldman, *What We Owe Iraq*, 40, 140 n. 32.

31. On the period, see Janet Afary, *The Iranian Constitutional Revolution, 1906–1911* (New York: Columbia University Press, 1996).

32. In the Tobacco Rebellion of 1891–93, the scholars supported the merchants after the shah "granted a monopoly on the production and sale of tobacco to a British entrepreneur." The scholars prohibited smoking, and, faced with this challenge, the shah backed down and revoked the monopoly. Bulliet, *The Case*, 72.

33. On the debate and the eventual contribution of Muhammad Husayn Na'ini, see Hamid Algar, "The Oppositional Role of the Ulama in Twentieth Century Iran," in Keddie, *Scholars, Saints, and Sufis*, 237–40. For an early mention of *mashru'eh*, see Said Arjomand, *The Turban for the Crown: The Islamic Revolution in Iran* (Oxford: Oxford University Press, 1988), 37–40.

34. On the drafting process, see Janet Afary, "Civil Liberties and the Making of Iran's First Constitution," *Comparative Studies of South Asia, Africa and the Middle East* 25, no. 2 (2005): 341.

35. The 1906 document, drafted and adopted under the dying Mozaffar al-Din Shah, was largely secular. His son and heir, Muhammad 'Ali Shah, took power in January 1907 and, with the assistance of conservative scholar Fazlollah Nuri, presided over the drafting and adoption of the 1907 supplementary laws that made Twelver Shi'ism the official religion and created a council of scholars to review legislation. See Afary, "Civil Liberties and the Making of Iran's First Constitution," 350, 354.

36. The supplementary law of October 1907, art. ii, states:

At no time must any legal enactment of the Sacred National Consultative Assembly ... be at variance with the sacred principles of Islam or the laws established by [the Prophet Muhammad].... It is hereby declared that it is for the learned doctors of theology [i.e., the scholars] to determine whether such laws as may be proposed are or are not conformable to the principles of Islam; and it is therefore officially enacted that there shall at all times exist a Committee composed of not less than five mujtahids or other devout theologians, cognizant also of the requirements of the age, in this manner. The [scholars] and Proofs of Islam shall present to the National Consultative Assembly the names of twenty of the ulema possessing the attributes mentioned above; and the Members of the National Consultative Assembly shall, either by unanimous acclamation, or by vote, designate five or more of these, according to the exigencies of the time, and recognize these as Members, so that they may carefully discuss and consider all matters proposed in the Assembly, and reject and repudiate, wholly or in part, any such proposal which is at variance with the Sacred Laws of Islam, so that it shall not obtain the title of legality. In such matters the decision of this Ecclesiastical Committee shall be followed and obeyed, and this article shall continue unchanged until the appearance of the [Hidden Imam].

37. Afary, "Civil Liberties and the Making of Iran's First Constitution," 354, simply notes that no parallel provision exists in the Belgian, Ottoman, and Bulgarian constitutions that provided models.

38. And Iran had not been colonized, so that any knowledge of British colonial supervisory practices, which used repugnancy clauses to ensure that local laws could be overridden when repugnant to British notions of equity and natural justice, would have been thirdhand at best. It would, of course, have been necessary to substitute the shari'a for equity and natural justice in the formulation. The framers did not list British colonial practices of respecting or rejecting local "native" laws among their sources of comparison—see Afary, "Civil Liberties and the Making of Iran's First Constitution," 349 n. 39—but it is not altogether impossible that contacts with Muslim scholars living under the Raj might have been a source of influence. The repugnancy clause of the 1956 constitution of Pakistan, since carried through to later versions, was certainly influenced by the Iranian model of 1907. Indeed, the drafting committee initially recommended the creation of a board of five 'ulama to determine whether any pending law "was repugnant to the Holy Quran or Sunnah." Kennedy, "Repugnancy to Islam," 770. The extent of British legal influence on the language of repugnancy is uncertain. See Ahmad, "Activism of the Ulama in Pakistan," 265–66.

39. See Keddie, "The Ulama's Power in Modern Iran," 211 (observing that "modern Iranian ulama [have] exercised so much more political power than the ulama of other Middle Eastern countries"). And Keddie was writing even before the Islamic revolution of 1979.

40. Algar, "The Role of the Ulama," 246–47. Since Algar was writing before the Islamic revolution of 1979, his account is free of anachronism.

41. Khomeini made regular use of the term *mustadafin*, a Qur'anic word for the downtrodden that took on resonances of Frantz Fanon's *damnés de la terre* via the intercession of 'Ali Shari'ati.

42. Arjomand, *The Turban for the Crown*, 154.

43. The Mojahedin-i-Khalq, with their combination of Islamism and radical leftist ideology, were destroyed by 1982. Ibid.

44. Ibid., vi.

45. Cf. Plato, *Statesman*, 296 et seq.

46. Robert Nozick, *Anarchy, State, and Utopia* (New York: Basic Books, 1974), 12–25.

47. Quentin Wictorowicz, *The Management of Islamic Activism: Salafis, the Muslim Brotherhood, and State Power in Jordan* (Albany: SUNY Press, 2001).

Conclusion

1. See, for example, the Cairo Declaration on Judicial Independence in the Arab Region, produced by the Second Arab Justice conference, "Supporting and Promoting the Independence of the Judiciary." February 21–24, 2003.

INDEX

Abbas, Mahmoud, 141
Abbasids, 36–40, 157n5
Abdulhamid II, 7, 76–77, 78, 124
Abdulmecid I, 59
absolutism, 60–61. *See also* executive
Abu Bakr, 25
administrative regulations: authority of ruler to issue, 64; and criminal justice system, 49; in Ottoman Empire, 42–44, 53, 61, 70, 115; and Saudi king, 96; and scholars, 50, 51, 61, 62; and shari'a, 46; sultan's power beyond, 77
Afghanistan, 105, 111, 123, 144; constitution of 2004, 11, 12, 14, 121, 127, 133; and Iranian constitution, 133; as Islamic state, 2; Taliban in, 137–38
Africa, 89, 90, 139
AK Party (Adalet ve Kalkinma Partisi), 143
Algeria, 59, 88, 105, 141, 142, 145
'Ali ibn Abi Talib, 128, 129
Andalusia, 44–45
Arabia, 53, 92, 93
Arab nationalism, 87
Arab Revolt, 94–95

Arabs/Arab world, 53, 54, 80, 85, 88, 90–91, 92, 142–43
Arab states, 118, 141
Aristotle, 130–31
Armenians, 78
Asia, 89
Ataturk. *See* Kemal Pasha (Ataturk)
Austro-Hungarian Empire, 73
autocracy: and Abdulhamid, 78; and displacement of scholars, 91; failure of secular, 6; and Iran, 147; and Islamism, 112–13, 142, 144; and Ottoman reforms, 60–61, 69; reform of, 149; of Saddam Hussein, 148. *See also* dictatorships; executive
ayatollah, 130

Bahrain, 141
balance of powers: between caliph and scholars, 28, 29; and Ibn Khaldun, 42; in Iran, 137; in Islamic constitution, 6, 40, 74, 90; and Islamism, 15; in Ottoman reforms, 77
Bani-Sadr, Abo'l-Hasan, 135
Banna, Hassan al-, 107
Belgian constitution, 132, 133
Bentham, Jeremy, 75

177